Congratulations!
13
WITCH POWERS
ACTIVATED!

D1441416

How will you use these powers?
What's next for you?!

COLORING BOOK OF SHADOWS

Planner for A Magical

2024

AMY CESARI

Be a fire-safe witch!

Lots of space above and around the flame.

Candle is on a fire-safe dish.

Never leave flames unattended.

- Thirteen Powers -

This book will take you through twelve spells to "unlock" or show you the depths of your witch powers. You've already got the most important (the thirteenth...) so go ahead and check that off below. *Check!*

13
THE POWER OF YOU

You've already got this!
☐

01
DESIRE
Claim what you want.
☐

02
SHADOW
Find what you've hidden.
☐

03
INTENTION
Take action & believe.
☐

04
THE MIND
Follow your intuition.
☐

05
EARTH
Feel that you belong.
☐

06
FIRE
Know that you can change.
☐

- Unlock Them All! -

As you do each spell in the book and "feel" the power it describes, check off the boxes below. At the end of the year (or sooner if you're an overachiever!), you'll find you've activated your full witch power.

07
WATER
Feel your emotions.
☐

08
AIR
Know what you think.
☐

09
SPIRIT
Know your soul's magic.
☐

10
PROTECTION
Create your space.
☐

11
BANISHING
Release & let things go.
☐

12
ENERGY
Know you're limitless.
☐

Magic?! You've Got This.

The most widely accepted definition of magic is the ability to influence your destiny. To align your intention, will, and the natural forces around you—such as the moon, the sun, the planets, and the changing seasons—is magic.

Magic is like an invisible thread. You may barely notice it's there at times. But if you hang onto that thread of intention (and action) through the many moons and phases of your year, that magic will come through for you in life-changing ways.

This book isn't about planning to do more, but about prioritizing magic in your life and pulling that thread forward, amidst the ups and downs.

You've already got what you need to make this year magical. Are you ready? *Say yes!*

You're capable and ready for it.

You may already be familiar with the 12 "witch powers" in this book. If you are, that's great news, because it means you're ready to strengthen your connection to magic as you work through these spells, and unlock new levels of witch power.

If these powers are new to you, you'll likely feel a hint of recognition as you do the work, as if you're remembering a "lost" magic from your past. And if not? If magic feels new to you, cherish these first emerging moments of your powers—they are potent.

So are you ready to feel that magic?! Rub your hands together till you feel energy move down your arms, to your spine, and through your body. Then hold your palms out and say, "The magic is mine!" (and cackle maniacally if you wish!).

You'll feel that spark, because your "witch powers" are already within you, just waiting to be activated. So consider this your invitation and permission slip to believe in the power of you... and your capacity to make real magic happen.

Believing in your magic means knowing that you are capable. You've plunged into darkness many times before, and you've weathered a few storms... yes? Knowing that, you can believe in yourself and believe in your magic to make things happen.

So, say yes to what you desire, to what you wish to change, and to the magic of the dark, the light, and everything in-between. Your witch powers are always there for you, and they will help you navigate your journey through life.

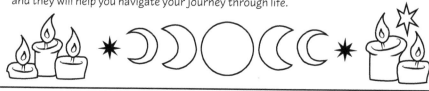

Wield Thy Power! THE MAGIC Is Yours.

TIPS TO USE THIS PLANNER

1. Familiarize yourself with the introduction and basics of magic and spellcasting.
2. Fill out the "MAGICAL VISION" planning pages at the end of the introduction.
3. Try to perform the "big spell" or one of the mini-spells in this book each month.
4. Review your MAGICAL VISION monthly, whenever you like, or on the new moon. Adjust as needed, then break your goals into smaller intentions and actions for the month, and try to keep moving forward. Step by step.
5. Repeat this process for as many of the 12 months of the year as you can to "stir the cauldron"... and see what happens. (It'll be magic!)

• There is only one rule: you're not allowed to stress about "keeping up" on coloring the whole book. Enjoy the parts you do color *if any*, and don't worry about the rest.
• Since this book is printed on both sides of the page, it works best if you use colored pencils, crayons, or ballpoint pens. Markers will bleed through to the other side.
• Write, color, and draw in this book! Take notes. Expressing your thoughts in writing is a powerful way to create your reality. Here are some ideas of what to write: *Your day-to-day-mundane appointments. Daily gratitude. Daily reflections. Daily tarot. A diary of your spiritual journey. Intuitive messages. How you feel during different moon phases.*
• "Spellcasting Basics" are included to show you how to cast a circle, ground and center, and perform a "full" spell. If you are new to spells, please be sure to read this.
•And remember, the magic is inside you. Even if you start this book "late" or if it's not "the best" moon phase for a spell, you are the real power behind your magical life.

GOALS, PLANS, AND INTENTIONS

Yes, this is a planner, but that doesn't mean you have to get intense about... planning. You can even plan to do less this year. In fact, that's a great idea. Get to know what *you* want (not your family, not society, etc... .) and then use the powers of magic and intention to focus your energy on those things. Here are some tips:
• Less is more. Go for broader feelings and intentions rather than super specific dates, processes, and outcomes. Leave room for magic to surprise you in fantastic ways.
• Make your goals as big or small as you want.
• Instead of saying what you don't want, "to stop being an emotional wreck," phrase it positively so you feel good when you say it, "to feel at ease with all of my emotions."
• Any plans you make are more of a guideline. Don't be afraid to scrap them and do something else if they don't feel right anymore. It's never too late to change directions or make new plans—in fact, that's often where the real magic comes into play.

HOW TO DO Magic

THE COSMOS
... and all things outside of your "control" ...

....LIKE OTHER PEOPLE & OUTSIDE INFLUENCES.

How do you use magic in real life?! By "stirring the cauldron" in your sphere of influence. Intention is the strongest magical power that you have. Simply put, intention means focusing your desire and energies towards what you want.

Since you're a powerful witch, you're always creating your reality. *So is it all your fault?!* No. Absolutely not. You're not the only one putting out energy and intentions. Everyone is. And our planes of reality are constantly feeling the influence of "outside" energies. Lots of stuff happens that you had no intention of creating.

Does that mean you're helpless against these outside forces? *Nope!* Outside influences are strong. But guess what... your sphere of influence is mighty strong, too. And you can also find ways to work with outside influences (like Astrology).

It's your job (if you choose to accept it!) to stir the contents of your own cauldron of intention toward what you desire. The illustration on the

DIVINE

PSYCHIC

MENTAL

EMOTIONAL

Stir That Cauldron!

PHYSICAL REALM

Your sphere of influence

right-hand page showcases your powers.

The physical realm is your body, your home, your stuff, and your spellcasting ingredients like herbs and candles. The emotional realm is your frequency that vibrates with your feelings. The mental realm is the energy of your thoughts. The psychic realm is interconnectedness, where you send out all of these energies into the universe and where you receive intuitive guidance and knowledge. And the divine realm is the level of universal or divine consciousness, your true self, your soul, and connectedness with "all" that is.

So, what do you do with this? Keep stirring your "cauldron" and aligning your intention, energies, and actions towards your desired outcome.

You'll go deeper into all of these powers as this book progresses, but for now, start noticing your actions, emotions, thoughts, intuitive guidance, and the calling of your soul. Then keep stirring your cauldron toward what you desire.

SPELLCASTING

TO SEE
Candles illuminate situations and spells.

to Release
& BANISH
Scissors, flames, and burying things in the earth release energy.

TO GROW
Your garden and your imagination can help energy grow in spells.

To Create
Enliven the energy of what you wish to create with fiery spells and rituals.

TO ATTRACT
Similar energy attracts! Use your own vibration as well as the energy of crystals "charged" with your intentions.

TO CLEAR & CLEANSE
Bathing, sweeping, and moving energy with air or smoke can amplify your intentions of clearing and cleansing.

& INTENTIONS

TO EMPOWER

Crystals, wands, and the power of your own hands, body, and actions can empower your spells.

to Listen

Use tarot cards, gaze at reflective surfaces, and most importantly, feel and listen very closely to your emotions and energetic body.

TO HEAL

Sewing, mending, and accepting what's passed will help to heal.

To Protect

Use herbs, circles, and symbols of knots and "unbroken" lines to protect your energy.

TO SEEK

Reading, listening, and asking "to know" will provide the answers you seek.

To Know

Intuitive wisdom is already yours. Feel for the knowing in your body.

To Wish

Gaze at the moon, the stars, and most of all, believe that your dreams and desires can come true.

TYPES OF SPELLS

GARDEN

Visualization

BLESSING

Altar & SACRED SPACE

DIRECTING ENERGY

Candles & FIRE

BATHING

Art

& RITUAL IDEAS

Not a complete list. Add your own!

Intention

INCENSE

Sewing

KITCHEN & TEA

Herbs

EXPERIENCING NATURE & THE COSMOS

Writing

THE ELEMENTS

SPIRIT

CONNECTION TO THE DIVINE SOURCE, DIVINE WITHIN, OR TRUE SELF.

WATER

EMOTION, INTUITION, AND CLEANSING RELEASE.

AIR

KNOWLEDGE, IDEAS, EXPANSION, AND COMMUNICATION.

EARTH

BELONGING, SECURITY, AND ABUNDANCE OF RESOURCES.

FIRE

CREATIVITY, LOVE, INSPIRATION, DESTROYING TO RE-CREATE.

- and the -
THE PENTACLE

THE ZODIAC

Capricorn (10)
"ACTIVE PRACTICALITY"
RULED BY SATURN.
STRUCTURED & FOCUSED.
SUN: DEC. 22–JAN. 19

Sagittarius (9)
"ADAPTABLE ENTHUSIASM"
RULED BY JUPITER.
EXPLORATORY & ENLIGHTENING.
SUN: NOV. 22–DEC. 21

Aquarius (11)
"DETERMINED INTELLECTUAL"
RULED BY URANUS.
ECCENTRIC & HUMANITARIAN.
SUN: JAN. 20–FEB. 18

Scorpio (8)
"DETERMINED FEELINGS"
RULED BY PLUTO.
TRANSFORMATIVE & SPIRITUAL.
SUN: OCT. 23–NOV. 21

Pisces (12)
"ADAPTABLE FEELINGS"
RULED BY NEPTUNE.
CREATIVE, DREAMY, & SENSITIVE.
SUN: FEB. 19–MAR. 20

Libra (7)
"ACTIVE INTELLECTUAL"
RULED BY VENUS.
BALANCED, SOCIAL, & FAIR.
SUN: SEPT. 23–OCT. 22

Aries (1)
"ACTIVE INSPIRATION"
RULED BY MARS.
AMBITIOUS & MOTIVATED.
SUN: MAR. 21–APRIL 19

Virgo (6)
"ADAPTABLE PRACTICALITY"
RULED BY MERCURY.
DETAILED & ORGANIZED.
SUN: AUG. 23–SEPT. 22

Taurus (2)
"DETERMINED PRACTICALITY"
RULED BY VENUS.
COMFORTABLE & GROUNDED.
SUN: APRIL 20–MAY 20

Leo (5)
"PERSISTENT ENTHUSIASM"
RULED BY THE SUN.
CREATIVE, BOLD, & PASSIONATE.
SUN: JULY 23–AUG. 22

Gemini (3)
"ADAPTABLE INTELLECT"
RULED BY MERCURY.
COMMUNICATIVE & RESILIENT.
SUN: MAY 21–JUNE 20

Cancer (4)
"ACTIVE FEELINGS"
RULED BY THE MOON.
INTROSPECTIVE & INTUITIVE.
SUN: JUNE 21–JULY 22

THE SECRETS OF

YOUR FEELINGS ARE THE SECRET SAUCE

To make real magic happen, combine actions (things that you do), intentions (also known as feelings or emotions), as well as powers outside of yourself, such as the moon and nature. This chart will give you some ideas on how to feel and set your intentions.

An intention is when you strongly feel what you desire in your body, as if you already have it.

You can use the phases of the moon to "pull the thread" of magic forward by listening to your feelings and continually refocusing these intentions with actions to match.

Since the moon and emotions are both linked to the subconscious, *you'll use your body to feel these things and set intentions*, not your thoughts in your conscious mind.

FIRST QUARTER

Feel where you would like to change, grow, or expand. Allow yourself to dream and imagine what it might be like to make a change, even if it doesn't seem possible right now.

WAXING CRESCENT

Feel what excites you and sparks a sense of curiosity. Ask questions and look for answers, clues, patterns, and coincidences. Use the subtle feelings of what "lights you up" to set intentions and guide your actions.

NEW MOON

Allow yourself to feel where you are judging yourself. When you are ready, forgive yourself and let the energy shift until you find a place of neutrality and self-acceptance.

MOON MAGIC

FULL MOON

Reaffirm your visions and intentions until the energy of what you desire begins to feel real.
If you feel clarity, make decisions to move forward quickly.
If you feel confusion, illuminate your emotions through writing, ritual, divination, movement, etc.
Ask: What am I missing? What am I feeling?

LAST QUARTER

Allow yourself to feel what's working, and what isn't. Let your feelings flow to a place of ease and trust in yourself, so you can discern what you want and what you do not want.

WANING CRESCENT

Feel the relief as you realize that some thoughts and feelings are unnecessary. Intend to let those things go, and then see what you have left. Let your intentions flow to a place of release.

DARK

Let the darkness filter out noise and distractions. Take a step back from actions and thoughts. Allow the dark moon to reset your mind, body, and spirit with the energy of rest.

the correspondence of
THE MOON AND SEASONS

The moon completes a full cycle of its phases in just over 28 days, which is relatively quick. One moon cycle is perfect for shorter projects and immediate goals.

You can also "correspond" these shorter moon phases to a longer-term cycle, the seasons, also known as the Wheel of the Year. This longer cycle is useful for "big" goals and plans that'll take more than a month.

While the seasons and sun embody more of a conscious or outward energy, the moon is subconscious or internal. However, they both follow a similar cycle and progression of dark to light.

The handy chart on the following page demonstrates that the phases of the moon correspond to an energy point on the Wheel of the Year. This pattern of energy—the waxing and waning of light—is no coincidence. It's the pattern and flow of the creative force of the universe. This process and cycle is how magic "works."

Here's an overview of the eight sabbats and a chart that connects them to the moon phases and seasons.

IMBOLC: February 1 or 2. Imbolc is the time to celebrate the first signs of spring or the return of the sun's increasing light. This sabbat corresponds to the waxing crescent moon.

OSTARA: March 20. This sabbat is celebrated on the spring equinox. Witches often mark this day with a ritual planting of seeds. Ostara corresponds to the first quarter moon.

BELTANE: May 1. Beltane is a time for rituals of growth, creation, and taking action to make things happen. This sabbat corresponds to the waxing gibbous moon.

LITHA: June 20. This sabbat celebrates the summer solstice, when the sun is at its strongest. Litha is a time of great magical and personal power and corresponds to the full moon.

LUGHNASADH: August 1. This day is a celebration of the "first harvest" where we gather early grains, herbs, fruits, and vegetables from the earth. It corresponds to the waning gibbous moon, where light and power begin to descend from their fullest stage.

MABON: September 21. Celebrated on the autumnal equinox, this sabbat is about release, balance, and letting go. It is the second harvest and corresponds to the last quarter moon.

SAMHAIN: October 31. Samhain is a celebration of the dark half of the year. It is a time to cast spells of protection for the upcoming winter. It corresponds to the waning crescent moon.

YULE: December 21. Marked by the winter solstice and the shortest (darkest) day of the year, this sabbat corresponds to the dark and new moon.

A NOTE ABOUT THE CROSS-QUARTER DATES AND SOUTHERN HEMISPHERE SEASONS:

CROSS QUARTER DATES: The dates for the two solstices and two equinoxes each year—Ostara, Litha, Mabon, and Yule—are calculated astronomically, from the position of the earth to the sun. The "cross quarter" festivals, which are the points between—Imbolc, Beltane, Lughnasadh, and Samhain—are often celebrated on "fixed" dates instead of the actual midpoints. This book lists both the "Fixed Festival Dates," where it's more common to celebrate, and the "Astronomical Dates." Choose either date or any time in between for your own ritual. 'Tis the season for magic.

SOUTHERN HEMISPHERE SEASONS: If you're on the "southern" half of the Earth, like in Australia, the seasonal shifts are opposite on the calendar year. So you'll feel the energy of the summer solstice (corresponding to the full moon) in December instead of June, and so on.

Spellcasting Basics

There are opening and closing steps that are basic accompaniments to spells in this book. These steps are optional but advisable: at least know "why" many witches perform these processes and try them out for yourself.

And keep in mind, this is a super basic "coloring book" guide to the spellcasting process. There are books and online sources that go much further in-depth.

THE SECRET OF SPELLS

The secret to powerful spells is in you. Your feeling and vibration in alignment with your true source of self—and/or a higher power—is what makes spells work.

The secret isn't in having the right ingredients and doing all the steps in a particular order. It's in your ability to focus your intent and use your feelings, mind, and soul to call in what you want—to harness the energy of yourself in harmony with the Earth, stars, moon, planets, or whatever other spiritual forces you call upon.

BREAK THE RULES

The first rule is to throw out any of the rules that don't work for you. Do things that feel right, significant, and meaningful. Adapt spells from different practices, books, and teachers. The only way to know what works is to follow your curiosity and try things out.

USING TOOLS

Your feelings and vibration are what unlocks the magic, not the tools, exact words, or sequences. You can cast amazing spells for free with no tools at all, and you can cast an elaborate spell that yields no results.

That said, tools like herbs, oils, crystals, and cauldrons can be powerful and fun to use in your spells. Just don't feel pressured or discouraged if you don't have much to start. Keep your magic straightforward and powerful. The right tools and ingredients will come.

"AS ABOVE, SO BELOW"

Tools, ingredients, and symbols are based on the magical theory of sympathetic magic and correspondence. You might hear the phrase, "As Above, So Below," which means the spiritual qualities of objects are passed down to earth. It's "sympathetic magic," or "this equals that," like how a figure of a lion represents that power but is not an actual lion.

Start by following lists, charts, and spells to get a feel for what others use and then begin to discover your own meaningful symbolism and correspondences.

PERMISSION

Spellbooks are like guidelines. They should be modified, simplified, or· embellished to your liking. And don't degrade your magic by calling it "lazy." Keeping your witchcraft simple is okay. Go ahead, you have permission.

Also, it's not a competition to see who can use the most esoteric stuff in their spell. Hooray! It's about finding your personal power and style.

SPELLCASTING OUTLINE:

1. Plan and prepare.
2. Cast a circle.
3. Ground and center.
4. Invoke a deity or connection to self.
5. Raise energy.
6. Do your spellcraft (like the spells in this book).
7. Ground and center again.
8. Close your circle.
9. Clean up.
10. Act in accord (and be patient).

1. PLAN AND PREPARE: If you're doing a written spell, read it several times to get familiar with it. Decide if there's anything you'll substitute or change. If you're writing your own spell, enjoy the process and mystery of seeing the messages and theme come together.

Gather all of the items you'll be using (if any) and plan out the space and time where you'll do the spell. Spells can be impromptu, so preparations can be quick and casual if you like.

2. CAST A CIRCLE AND CALL THE QUARTERS: A magic circle is a container to collect the energy of your spell. Circles are also protective, as they form a ring or "barrier" around you. Circles can elevate your space to a higher vibration and clear out unwanted energy before you begin. Calling the Quarters is done to get the universal energies of the elements flowing. Incense is typically burned at the same time to purify the air and energy. If you

can't burn things, that's ok. If you've never cast a circle, try it. It's a mystical experience like no other. Once you have a few candles lit and start to walk around it, magic does happen!

HOW TO CAST A CIRCLE: This is a basic, bare-bones way to cast a circle. It's often much more elaborate, and this explanation barely does it justice, so read up to find out more. And note that while some cast the circle first and then call the Quarters, some do it the other way around.

1. Hold out your hand, wand, or crystal, and imagine a white light and a sphere of pure energy surrounding your space, as you circle around clockwise three times. Your circle can be large or it can be tiny, just space for you and your materials.

2. Call the Four Quarters or Five Points of the Pentagram, depending on your preferences. The Quarters (also known as the Elements!) are Earth (North), Air (East), Fire (South), and Water (West). Many use the Pentagram and also call the 5th Element, Spirit or Self.

Face in each direction and say a few words to welcome the element. For example, "To the North, I call upon the power of grounding and strength. To the East, I call upon the source of knowledge. To the South, I call upon the passion and burning desire to take action. To the West, I call upon the intuition of emotion. To the Spirit and Source of Self, I call upon the guidance and light."

3. GROUND AND CENTER: Grounding and centering prepare you to use the energy from the Earth, elements, and universe. Most witches agree that if you skip these steps, you'll be drawing off of your own energy, which can be exhausting and ineffective. It's wise to ground and center both before and after a spell. It's like the difference between being "plugged into" the magical energy of the Earth and universe versus "draining your batteries."

HOW TO GROUND AND CENTER:

To ground, imagine the energy coming up from the core of the Earth and into your feet, as you breathe deeply. You can visualize deep roots from your feet all the way into the center of the Earth, with these roots drawing the Earth's energy in and out of you. The point is to allow these great channels of energy to flow through you and into your spell. You can also imagine any of your negative energy, thoughts, or stress leaving.

To center, once you've got a good flow of energy from the ground, imagine the energy shining through and out the top of your head as a pure form of your highest creative self and then back in as the light of guidance. Suspend yourself here between the Earth and the sky, supported with the energy flowing freely through you, upheld, balanced, cleansed, and "in flow" with the energy of the universe. This process takes just a couple of minutes.

4. INVOKE A DEITY OR CREATIVE SOURCE: If you'd like to invoke a deity or your highest self to help raise energy and your vibration, call upon them. Invoking deities is way deeper than this book, so research it more if it calls to you!

5. RAISE ENERGY: The point of raising energy is to channel the universal (magical!) forces you tapped into through the previous steps to use in your spell. And raising energy is fun. You can sing, dance, chant, meditate, or do breath work. You want to do something that feels natural, so you can really get into it, lose yourself, and raise your state of consciousness.

A good way to start is to chant "Ong," allowing the roof of your mouth to vibrate ever so slightly. This vibration changes up the energy in your mind, body, and breath and is a simple yet powerful technique.

Another tip is to raise energy to the point of the "peak" where you feel it at its highest. Don't go too far where you start to tucker out or lose enthusiasm!

6. DO YOUR SPELL: Your spell can be as simple as saying an intention and focusing on achieving the outcome of what you want, or it can be more elaborate. Whichever way you prefer, do what feels right to you.

TIPS ON VISUALIZATION AND INTENTION:

Most spellwork involves a bit of imagination and intention, and here are some subtleties you can explore.

The Power of You The most important tool in magic is you. You've got it—both power right now and vast untapped power that you can explore. To cast a successful spell, you've got to focus your mind and genuinely feel the emotions and feelings of the things you want to manifest.

If you haven't started meditating in some form yet, start now! It's not too late, and it's easier than you think.

Visualize the Outcome

Visualization doesn't have to be visual. In fact, *feeling* the outcome of what you want may be more effective than seeing it (try both). And try to feel or see the *completion* of your desire without worrying about the process or *how* you'll get there.

If you don't know how you're going to achieve your goal (yet!), it can feel overwhelming when you try to visualize how you're going to pull it off. Instead, feel the sense of calm, completion, and control that you'll feel *after* you achieve it.

Phrase it Positively

Another tip is to phrase your intentions and desires positively. You're putting energy into this, so make sure the intention is going to be good for you. Instead of saying what you don't want, "to get out of my bad job that I hate," phrase it positively, "I want to do something that's fulfilling with my career."

Then you'll be able to feel good about it as you visualize and cast your spell.

7. GROUND AND CENTER AGAIN

After your spell, it's important to ground out any excess energy. Do this again by visualizing energy flowing through you and out. You can also imagine any "extra" energy you have petering out as you release it back into the Earth.

8. CLOSE YOUR CIRCLE

If you called the Quarters or a deity, let them know the spell has ended by calling them out again, with thanks if desired.

Close your circle the opposite of how you opened it, circling around three times or more counterclockwise. Then say, "This circle is closed," or do a closing chant or song to finish your spell.

9. CLEAN UP

Don't be messy with your magic! Put away all of your spell items.

10. ACT IN ACCORD: Once you have cast your spell, you've got to take action. You can cast a spell to become a marine biologist, but if you don't study for it, it's never going to happen. So take action towards what you want to open the possibility for it to come.

Look for signs, intuition, and coincidences that point you in the direction of your desires. If you get inspired after a spell, take action! Don't be surprised if you ask for money and then come up with a new idea to make money. Follow those clues, especially if they feel exciting and good.

If your spell comes true, discard and "release" any charm bag, poppet, or item you used to hold and amplify energy. Also, give thanks (if that's in your practice) or repay the universe in some way, doing something kind or of service that you feel is a solid trade for what you received from your spell.

WHAT IF YOUR SPELL DOESN'T WORK?

It's true that not all spells will work! But sometimes the results just take longer than you'd like, so be patient.

If your spell doesn't work, you can use divination or meditation to do some digging into reasons why.

The good news is your own magic, power, frequency, and intention is still on your side. You can try again and add more energy in the direction of your desired outcome by casting another spell.

Give it some deep thought. What else is at play? Did you really take inspired action? Are you totally honest with yourself about what you want? Are there any thoughts or feelings about your spell that feel "off"? Are you grateful for what you already have? Can you "give back" or reciprocate with service or energy?

FOR MORE TIPS AND INSPIRATION:

Seek out websites, books, podcasts, and videos on spirituality. Follow your intuition and curiosity to deepen your practice and find your own style. And check out other books in the *Coloring Book of Shadows* series, like the *Book of Spells* and *Witch Life*.

SOUTHERN HEMISPHERE MAGIC

If you're in the Southern Hemisphere in a place like Australia, there are a couple of differences that you'll need to note.

The biggest difference is that since seasonal shifts are opposite on the calendar year, you'll feel the energy of Samhain around May 1 instead of October 31.

Southern Hemisphere "spinning and circle casting" will go "sun wise" according to the south—counterclockwise for invoking (drawing in), clockwise for banishing (letting go).

North and South Elements are also typically swapped in Southern Hemisphere magic—North = Fire, South = Earth.

SO MOTE IT BE.

Your Magical Vision

AND PLANS FOR THIS YEAR:

Remember that plans almost always change. So try to envision what you can influence no matter what, and don't worry about deadlines. Magic works in its own time.

- Who do you want to be this year?
- What do you want this year to feel like?
- What do you want to take action on or work towards?
- What steps, thoughts, actions, and feelings will get you going in the direction that you desire?
- What does success feel and look like to you?
- What do you really want that you are hesitant to ask for?

Reach for the Stars

THINGS YOU CAN CONTROL: *Nothing!* You can't control anything, but you can influence, plan, and make things better for yourself and for the world. You matter, and your magic and energy matter.

THINGS YOU CAN INFLUENCE OR CHANGE: Your priorities, your actions, your thoughts, how you spend some of your time, the collective consciousness, and the spiritual evolution of the planet. Ultimately, you can influence how you feel after you've processed and felt all of your feelings just as they are.

So Below!

1ST HALF 2024

January

S	M	T	W	Th	F	Sa
	1	2	◑	4	5	6
7	8	9	10	●	12	13
14	15	16	◐	18	19	20
21	22	23	24	○	26	27
28	29	30	31			

February

S	M	T	W	Th	F	Sa
				1	◑	3
4	5	6	7	8	●	10
11	12	13	14	15	◐	17
18	19	20	21	22	23	○
25	26	27	28	29		

March

S	M	T	W	Th	F	Sa
					1	2
◑	4	5	6	7	8	9
●	11	12	13	14	15	16
◐	18	19	20	21	22	23
24	○	26	27	28	29	30
31						

April

S	M	T	W	Th	F	Sa
	◑	2	3	4	5	6
7	●	9	10	11	12	13
14	◐	16	17	18	19	20
21	22	○	24	25	26	27
28	29	30				

May

S	M	T	W	Th	F	Sa
			◑	2	3	4
5	6	●	8	9	10	11
12	13	14	◐	16	17	18
19	20	21	22	○	24	25
26	27	28	29	◑	31	

June

S	M	T	W	Th	F	Sa
						1
2	3	4	5	●	7	8
9	10	11	12	13	◐	15
16	17	18	19	20	○	22
23	24	25	26	27	◑	29
30						

2ND HALF 2024

July

S	M	T	W	Th	F	Sa
	1	2	3	4	●	6
7	8	9	10	11	12	◗
14	15	16	17	18	19	20
○	22	23	24	25	26	◗
28	29	30	31			

August

S	M	T	W	Th	F	Sa
				1	2	3
●	5	6	7	8	9	10
11	◖	13	14	15	16	17
18	○	20	21	22	23	24
25	◗	27	28	29	30	31

September

S	M	T	W	Th	F	Sa
1	●	3	4	5	6	7
8	9	10	◖	12	13	14
15	16	○	18	19	20	21
22	23	◗	25	26	27	28
29	30					

October

S	M	T	W	Th	F	Sa
		1	●	3	4	5
6	7	8	9	◖	11	12
13	14	15	16	○	18	19
20	21	22	23	◖	25	26
27	28	29	30	31		

November

S	M	T	W	Th	F	Sa
					●	2
3	4	5	6	7	8	◖
10	11	12	13	14	○	16
17	18	19	20	21	◖	23
24	25	26	27	28	29	30

December

S	M	T	W	Th	F	Sa
●	2	3	4	5	6	7
◖	9	10	11	12	13	14
○	16	17	18	19	20	21
◖	23	24	25	26	27	28
29	●	31				

Black candles attract light.

White candles reflect light.

THIS MONTH:

Mercury Retrograde Ends: January 2
New Moon in Capricorn: January 11
Sun enters Aquarius: January 20
Full Moon in Leo: January 25
Uranus Retrograde Ends: January 27

Work with aquamarine to reconnect to your inner power.

-Willow Broom-
Witch Power

-Star of the Muses-
Sacred Power
& Inspiration

Drink spicy teas
to enliven your
senses.

Burn
sandalwood
to empower
your spirit.

Wear a conical hat to
channel your power.

JANUARY

CLAIMING YOUR POWER

Feel a glimmer of your witch power by deciding
that it's possible for your dreams to come true.

Hold your breath. Make a wish. Count to three.

What does your heart desire?

Claiming Your Power
A Spell to Activate Your Magic

The first four spells in the book delve into your inner power. This power is all you need to make magic happen, and it's already within you.

PREPARE an optional sacred space. The only requirement is your own self and body, existing right now as you are. If you want to embellish: light candles, burn incense like bay, sage, clove, or lemon verbena, or drink ginger or peppermint tea. You can also hold a crystal like quartz, citrine, or amethyst to help you feel your magic.

CAST YOUR SPELL. With your hand over your heart, claim what you desire or who you wish to be. Make your wish*. Decide that you can have it, and that it is possible, even if there are many steps (or obstacles) before you get there.

When you make your wish, you'll feel a spark of energy, a glimmer inside of you. That is the spark of magic. Feel that internally, even if for a split-second, and you will spark the cauldron of magic that is within you and available to you anytime, anywhere, and in any circumstance.

Once you feel that spark, aim to sit with it for a moment. Feel it flowing to you and through you, from the ground up through your body and out of the top of your head.

Repeat this spell anytime you feel lost or disconnected from your magic and intentions.

The next steps to make magic happen are to flow and "dance" with this energy as it manifests... which you'll do in the following spells.

*Aww, sorry! You can't wish people back from the dead or make someone specific fall in love with you. Your wish must comply with the laws of physics, biology, and free will for it to come true.

JANUARY 2024

	SUNDAY	MONDAY	TUESDAY
	31	1	2
	7	8	9
	14	15	16
	21	22	23
	28	29	30

-Charoite-

INTENTIONS
Claim Your Desire for Magic.

-Vervain-

WEDNESDAY	THURSDAY	FRIDAY	SATURDAY
3 Last Quarter ◑	4	5	6
10	11 New Moon ●♑	12	13
			☉ Sun in Aquarius ♒
17 First Quarter ◐	18	19	20
24	25 Full Moon ○ ♌	26	27
	★ Imbolc (Fixed Date)		
31	1	2 Last Quarter ◑	3

JANUARY 2024

MONDAY, JANUARY 1

TUESDAY, JANUARY 2
► Moon void-of-course begins 6:36 PM EST
Moon enters Libra ♎ 7:47 PM EST
☿℞ Mercury Retrograde ends

WEDNESDAY, JANUARY 3
Last Quarter ◑ 10:30 PM EST

THURSDAY, JANUARY 4

FRIDAY, JANUARY 5
► Moon void-of-course begins 6:41 AM EST
Moon enters Scorpio ♏ 7:39 AM EST

SATURDAY, JANUARY 6

SUNDAY, JANUARY 7
► Moon void-of-course begins 3:22 PM EST
Moon enters Sagittarius ♐ 4:08 PM EST

Hold citrine to your heart or solar plexus
to know your desires and inner wisdom.

JANUARY 2024

MONDAY, JANUARY 8

TUESDAY, JANUARY 9
►Moon void-of-course begins 1:25 PM EST
Moon enters Capricorn ♑ 8:33 PM EST

WEDNESDAY, JANUARY 10

THURSDAY, JANUARY 11
New Moon ● ♑ 6:57 AM EST
►Moon void-of-course begins 9:33 PM EST
Moon enters Aquarius ♒ 10:01 PM EST

FRIDAY, JANUARY 12

SATURDAY, JANUARY 13
►Moon void-of-course begins 4:59 AM EST
Moon enters Pisces ♓ 10:29 PM EST

SUNDAY, JANUARY 14

INNER POWER

Use an elder wand or broom to feel a sense of empowerment

JANUARY 2024

MONDAY, JANUARY 15
▸Moon void-of-course begins 11:33 PM EST
Moon enters Aries ♈ 11:49 PM EST

TUESDAY, JANUARY 16

WEDNESDAY, JANUARY 17
First Quarter ◑ 10:53 PM EST

THURSDAY, JANUARY 18
▸Moon void-of-course begins 3:03 AM EST
Moon enters Taurus ♉ 3:12 AM EST

FRIDAY, JANUARY 19

SATURDAY, JANUARY 20
▸Moon void-of-course begins 8:57 AM EST
Moon enters Gemini ♊ 8:58 AM EST
☉ Sun enters Aquarius ♒ 9:07 AM EST

SUNDAY, JANUARY 21

*Light a black or purple candle
and intend to learn something
new and valuable about magic.*

JANUARY 2024

MONDAY, JANUARY 22
►Moon void-of-course begins 3:40 PM EST
Moon enters Cancer ♋ 4:51 PM EST

TUESDAY, JANUARY 23

WEDNESDAY, JANUARY 24
►Moon void-of-course begins 5:58 PM EST

THURSDAY, JANUARY 25
Moon enters Leo ♌ 2:37 AM EST
Full Moon ○ ♌ 12:57 PM EST

FRIDAY, JANUARY 26
►Moon void-of-course begins 4:19 PM EST

SATURDAY, JANUARY 27
Moon enters Virgo ♍ 2:11 PM EST
♅℞ Uranus Retrograde ends

SUNDAY, JANUARY 28

CAT

*Channel cat energy
to focus your
witch power.*

JANUARY 2024/FEBRUARY 2024

MONDAY, JANUARY 29
►Moon void-of-course begins 6:20 PM EST

TUESDAY, JANUARY 30
Moon enters Libra ♎ 3:04 AM EST

WEDNESDAY, JANUARY 31

THURSDAY, FEBRUARY 1
★ Imbolc (Fixed Festival Date)
►Moon void-of-course begins 4:03 AM EST
Moon enters Scorpio ♏ 3:37 PM EST

FRIDAY, FEBRUARY 2
Last Quarter ☽ 6:18 PM EST

SATURDAY, FEBRUARY 3
►Moon void-of-course begins 10:24 PM EST

SUNDAY, FEBRUARY 4
Moon enters Sagittarius ♐ 1:28 AM EST
★ Imbolc (Astronomical Date) 3:28 AM EST

IMBOLC

Feel the magic of a fresh start. Try bathing or cleaning with enlivening herbs (basil or mint) and purifying herbs (agrimony and witch hazel.)

CROCUS

*Visualize (or feel)
a renewal of your
spirit and self.*

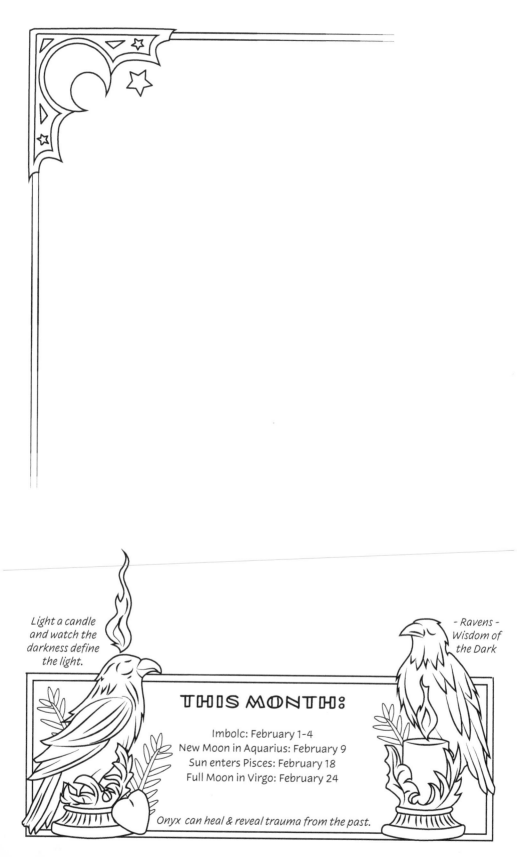

*Light a candle
and watch the
darkness define
the light.*

*- Ravens -
Wisdom of
the Dark*

THIS MONTH:

Imbolc: February 1-4
New Moon in Aquarius: February 9
Sun enters Pisces: February 18
Full Moon in Virgo: February 24

Onyx can heal & reveal trauma from the past.

- Magic Hexagram -
The polarity of light
and dark.

Burn rosemary
to recall who
you are.

Make a list of
dreams yet to be
fulfilled.

Carry a silver key to
unlock lost joy.

- Labradorite -
Self-Discovery

Protect your space with birch
incense or a birch broom.

Place thistles on your altar to
guide your shadow work.

FEBRUARY

POWER OF SHADOW

Rediscover the magic of your shadows
through intuition and self-acceptance.
Allow your secret desires to come to light.

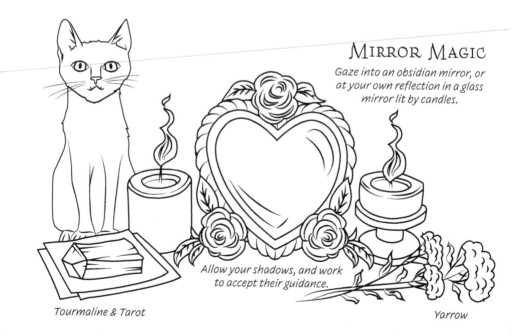

MIRROR MAGIC

Gaze into an obsidian mirror, or at your own reflection in a glass mirror lit by candles.

Allow your shadows, and work to accept their guidance.

Tourmaline & Tarot

Yarrow

Facing Your Shadow
Finding Power in the Darkness

When you think about who you are and what you desire, there might be a bit of "yeah, but...!" in the back of your mind. This tiny voice of doubt is shadowy gold—it points directly to a vital part of yourself that you are hesitant to face.

In shadow work, you might uncover false beliefs about why you can't have what you truly desire, or maybe you'll see possibilities you've hidden because of shame or fear.

For example, "art" as a shadow could mean you're afraid you're not good enough to be an artist. You might have given up on art and may be jealous of others. The point is to uncover and accept these desires without judgment or shame.

CAST THE SPELL: At midnight, light a black candle behind you and gaze into a mirror so you see the candle. Or just sit in near-total darkness.

Then answer the following questions (record and play them back on your phone if it's dark!).

1. What do you desire that you think you cannot have?

2. Why do you think you cannot have it?

3. If it was possible for you, how could it be possible?

4. What do you have to accept for it to come true?

5. What do you have to forgive in yourself to accept that this desire is possible for you? Extra Credit of Darkness: Who or what are you jealous of?

Once you've uncovered a shadow, ask: what were you trying to protect yourself from by hiding this shadow, and why? Explain the reasons to your shadow self, and be honest.

Then come up with first steps on how you can gently reincorporate this shadow back into your life, if and when you are ready.

FEBRUARY 2024

	SUNDAY	MONDAY	TUESDAY
	28	29	30
	★ Imbolc 3:28 AM EST 4	5	6
	11	12	13
	⊙ Sun enters Pisces ♓ 18	19	20
	25	26	27

Ruby-Fuchite

Rose

WEDNESDAY	THURSDAY	FRIDAY	SATURDAY
31	★ Imbolc (Fixed Date) 1	2 Last Quarter ◑	3
7	8	9 New Moon ● ≈	10
14	15	16 First Quarter ◑	17
21	22	23	24 Full Moon ○ ♍
28	29	1	2

FEBRUARY 2024

MONDAY, FEBRUARY 5

TUESDAY, FEBRUARY 6
▸ Moon void of course begins 12:06 AM EST
Moon enters Capricorn ♑ 7:09 AM EST

WEDNESDAY, FEBRUARY 7

THURSDAY, FEBRUARY 8
▸ Moon void of course begins 2:52 AM EST
Moon enters Aquarius ♒ 8:59 AM EST

FRIDAY, FEBRUARY 9
▸ Moon void of course begins 5:59 PM EST
New Moon ● ♒ 5:59 PM EST

*Befriend your darkness
with licorice, chamomile,
and ginseng tea.*

SATURDAY, FEBRUARY 10
Moon enters Pisces ♓ 8:42 AM EST

SUNDAY, FEBRUARY 11

*Drink tea for self-love with dark
chocolate, mint, and marshmallow root.*

FEBRUARY 2024

MONDAY, FEBRUARY 12
► Moon void of course begins 7:31 AM EST
Moon enters Aries ♈ 8:26 AM EST

TUESDAY, FEBRUARY 13

WEDNESDAY, FEBRUARY 14
► Moon void of course begins 5:21 AM EST
Moon enters Taurus ♉ 10:02 AM EST

THURSDAY, FEBRUARY 15

FRIDAY, FEBRUARY 16
First Quarter ◐ 10:01 AM EST
► Moon void of course begins 10:01 AM EST
Moon enters Gemini ♊ 2:39 PM EST

SATURDAY, FEBRUARY 17

SUNDAY, FEBRUARY 18
► Moon void of course begins 10:21 PM EST
Moon enters Cancer ♋ 10:25 PM EST
☉ Sun enters Pisces ♓ 11:12 PM EST

DOG

*Channel dog energy
to accept yourself
just as you are.*

Smoky Quartz

FEBRUARY 2024

MONDAY, FEBRUARY 19

TUESDAY, FEBRUARY 20

WEDNESDAY, FEBRUARY 21
► Moon void of course begins 1:38 AM EST
Moon enters Leo ♌ 8:40 AM EST

THURSDAY, FEBRUARY 22
► Moon void of course begins 11:18 PM EST

FRIDAY, FEBRUARY 23
Moon enters Virgo ♍ 8:38 PM EST

Mugwort

SATURDAY, FEBRUARY 24
Full Moon ○ ♍ 7:30 AM EST

SUNDAY, FEBRUARY 25

- Black Witch Moth -
Messages from the Other Side

FEBRUARY/MARCH 2024

MONDAY, FEBRUARY 26
➤ Moon void of course begins 2:25 AM EST
Moon enters Libra ♎ 9:29 AM EST

TUESDAY, FEBRUARY 27
➤ Moon void of course begins 1:22 PM EST

WEDNESDAY, FEBRUARY 28
Moon enters Scorpio ♏ 10:09 P EST

THURSDAY, FEBRUARY 29

FRIDAY, MARCH 1

SATURDAY, MARCH 2
➤ Moon void of course begins 2:47AM EST
Moon enters Sagittarius ♐ 8:56 AM EST

SUNDAY, MARCH 3
Last Quarter ◑ 10:23 AM EST

NETTLE

*An all-purpose herb
for shadow work &
counter-magic.*

Drink green tea and ginseng for extra energy to take action.

THIS MONTH:

New Moon in Pisces: March 10
Ostara (Spring Equinox): March 19
Sun enters Aries: March 19
Full Moon in Libra: March 25
Lunar Eclipse: March 25

PISCES

ARIES

AQUARI PISCES ARIES TAURUS GEMINI CANCER LEO VIRGO LIBRA SCORPIO SAGITT

CAPRL SAGITT SCORPIO

- Triskellion -
The cycles of life,
death, and rebirth.

- Snake -
Transformation

Rub thyme oil on
your shoes for
courage.

Use an oak wand or broom
to cast strong intentions.

Burn bay leaves and candles
to empower your actions.

- Quartz -
Moving energy

MARCH

POWER OF INTENTION

Perform "The Crystal Dance" by dancing around
with crystals as you cast energetic intentions.
Amplify your intentions with movement and action.

Channel hawk energy
to focus and direct
your attention.

Follow the
MAGIC

CASTING YOUR INTENTIONS
THE DANCE OF MAKING MAGIC

The new moon and spring equinox are auspicious times for intention-setting rituals, but intentions aren't a one-time, instant thing. Once you've set an intention, you've got to "dance" or move with that energy and take some steps and actions to manifest it.

PREPARE: Gather the clues you've collected from the two previous spells. Think deeply about what you desire outwardly and in the shadows. What is your intention? Write it down.

PERFORM THE RITUAL: Set up a ritual space in way that feels natural to you. For example, hold a crystal or light a white candle with a silver chain around it to amplify your intentions.

In your third eye, deeply feel your intention. Envision it if you can, but more importantly, immerse yourself in the feeling or energy of

already having it. This is the feeling that you want to "lock in" so you can recall it later.

Spend a few minutes to deepen the sensation, then bring the feeling to the lower back of your head. If your neck gets tingly—awesome.

TAKE ONE ACTION: Your magical guidance (intuition) will always show you at least one step to take in the direction that you want to go. This next step is already in your physical realm and you already know what it is... so take that step. This is a nice reminder that you aren't pushing, you are flowing into what is already there.

HOLD THE ENERGY: It's okay to fall out of sync with the energy of your intentions, but do yourself a favor... reset those intentions by frequently recalling the feelings you generated in this ritual, and remember... You are a witch!

MARCH 2024

SUNDAY	MONDAY	TUESDAY
25	26	27
3 Last Quarter ◗	4	5
10 New Moon ● ♓	11	12
17 First Quarter ◑	18	19 ★Ostara (Spring Equinox) ⊙ Sun enters Aries ♈
24	25 Full Moon ○ ♎	26 ★Penumbral Lunar Eclipse
31	1 Last Quarter ◗	2

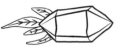

INTENTIONS
Visualize a Bright Future.

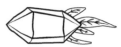

WEDNESDAY	THURSDAY	FRIDAY	SATURDAY
28	29	1	2
6	7	8	9
13	14	15	16
20	21	22	23
27	28	29	30
3	4	5	6

MARCH 2024

MONDAY, MARCH 4
▸ Moon void of course begins 10:41 AM EST
Moon enters Capricorn ♑ 4:15 PM EST

TUESDAY, MARCH 5

WEDNESDAY, MARCH 6
▸ Moon void of course begins 12:36 PM EST
Moon enters Aquarius ♒ 7:38 PM EST

THURSDAY, MARCH 7

FRIDAY, MARCH 8
▸ Moon void of course begins 1:56 PM EST
Moon enters Pisces ♓ 8:03 PM EST

SATURDAY, MARCH 9

SUNDAY, MARCH 10
New Moon ● ♓ 5:00 AM EDT
▸ Moon void of course begins 3:45 PM EDT
Moon enters Aries ♈ 8:19 PM EDT

*Burn incense with bergamot, goldenrod,
rose, and thyme for an uplifting boost.*

MARCH 2024

MONDAY, MARCH 11

TUESDAY, MARCH 12
► Moon void of course begins 7:08 AM EDT
Moon enters Taurus ♉ 8:28 PM EDT

WEDNESDAY, MARCH 13

THURSDAY, MARCH 14
► Moon void of course begins 6:29 PM EDT
Moon enters Gemini ♊ 11:16 PM EDT

FRIDAY, MARCH 15

SATURDAY, MARCH 16

SUNDAY, MARCH 17
First Quarter ◑ 12:11 AM EST
► Moon void of course begins 12:43 AM EDT
Moon enters Cancer ♋ 5:40 AM EDT

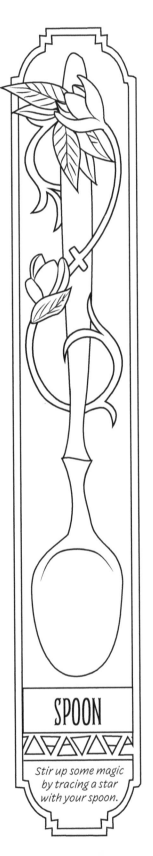

SPOON

Stir up some magic by tracing a star with your spoon.

MARCH 2024

MONDAY, MARCH 18

TUESDAY, MARCH 19
▸ Moon void of course begins 2:52 PM EDT
Moon enters Leo ♌ 3:33 PM EDT
★ Ostara (Spring Equinox) 11:07 PM EDT
☉ Sun enters Aries ♈ 11:06 PM EDT

WEDNESDAY, MARCH 20

THURSDAY, MARCH 21

FRIDAY, MARCH 22
▸ Moon void of course begins 2:34 AM EDT
Moon enters Virgo ♍ 3:42 AM EDT

SATURDAY, MARCH 23

SUNDAY, MARCH 24
▸ Moon void of course begins 11:49 AM EDT
Moon enters Libra ♎ 4:37 PM EDT

OSTARA

Feel the energy of exciting new possibilities.
Drink tea, burn incense, or bathe with herbs like
mugwort, rose, calendula, and jasmine.

MARCH 2024

MONDAY, MARCH 25
Full Moon ○ ♎ 3:00 AM EDT
Penumbral Lunar Eclipse 3:12 AM EDT

TUESDAY, MARCH 26
► Moon void of course begins 7:09 PM EDT

WEDNESDAY, MARCH 27
Moon enters Scorpio ♏ 5:03 AM EDT

THURSDAY, MARCH 28

FRIDAY, MARCH 29
► Moon void of course begins 11:40 AM EDT
Moon enters Sagittarius ♐ 3:52 PM EDT

SATURDAY, MARCH 30

SUNDAY, MARCH 31
► Moon void of course begins 8:16 PM EDT

- Lily of the Valley -
Lifting Your Spirits

Work with clary sage and owl energy to awaken the wisdom of your subconscious.

THIS MONTH:

Mercury Retrograde: April 1-25
New Moon in Aries: April 8
Total Solar Eclipse: April 8
Sun enters Taurus: April 19
Full Moon in Scorpio: April 23

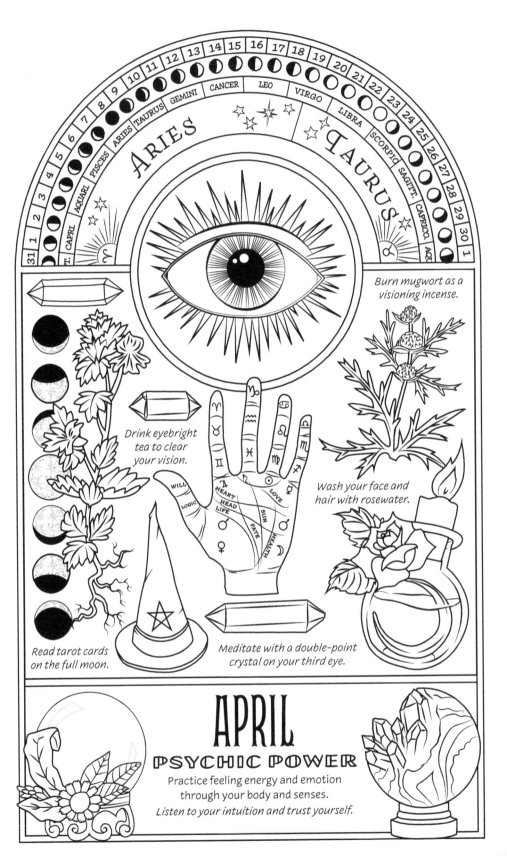

Burn mugwort as a visioning incense.

Drink eyebright tea to clear your vision.

Wash your face and hair with rosewater.

Read tarot cards on the full moon.

Meditate with a double-point crystal on your third eye.

APRIL
PSYCHIC POWER
Practice feeling energy and emotion through your body and senses.
Listen to your intuition and trust yourself.

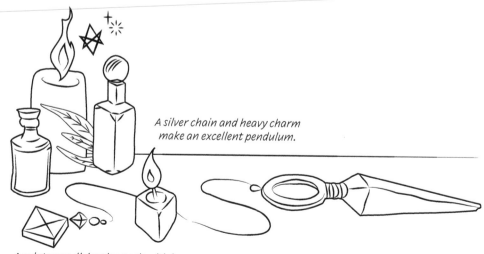

A silver chain and heavy charm make an excellent pendulum.

Anoint your divination tools with lemongrass oil to increase their psychic energy.

MIRROR OF THE MIND
PSYCHIC DEVELOPMENT

Everything has an energy or a "vibe," and "psychic power" is the ability to sense energy within yourself and outside of yourself. Psychic power is a pillar of magic, so practice often and see what happens when you trust your intuition.

THE STAIRCASE: A classic! Descend stairs in your mind's eye as you count down from ten to one (or try visualizing the spectrum of colors).

You'll find yourself in your subconscious mind or magic workshop. In that space, you can access your intuition and deepen your intentions.

TO SHARPEN YOUR SENSES: Ask yourself:

ENERGETIC SELF: What am I feeling in my gut? In my body? How does that compare to my thoughts? What am I sensing? What are my emotions? What is my vibe?

ENERGETICS OF OTHERS: Practice feeling or seeing the energy of other people, animals, plants, and objects. You might like to journey inside a crystal or plant in your mind's eye.

PHYSICAL SENSES: Touch different surfaces and notice their temperature. Try new spices and herbs, either by smelling or tasting. Look closely at shadows and light, and notice how light changes the color and mood of objects.

WORK WITH YOUR THOUGHTS: You can't control your thoughts, but you can work with them. Say/think, "I'm going to move my attention now," when you come across unwanted thoughts.

WORK WITH YOUR EMOTIONS: Feel the heck out of your emotions, even if they hurt. Name them out loud. Say where they are in your body and what they feel like. Then practice shifting to a different energy that you would prefer to feel.

APRIL 2024

	SUNDAY	MONDAY	TUESDAY
	31	1 Last Quarter ◐	2
	7	* Total Solar Eclipse 8 New Moon ● ♈	9
	14	15 First Quarter ◑	16
	21	22	23 Full Moon ○ ♏
	28	29	30

Violet

Aquamarine

INTENTIONS
Trust Your Intuition.

WEDNESDAY	THURSDAY	FRIDAY	SATURDAY
3	4	5	6
10	11	12	13
17	18	⊙ Sun enters Taurus 19	20
24	25	26	27
★ Beltane (Fixed Date) 1 Last Quarter ◑	2	3	★ Beltane 8:11 PM EDT 4

APRIL 2024

MONDAY, APRIL 1
Moon enters Capricorn ♑ 12:05 AM EDT
Last Quarter ◑ 11:15 PM EDT
☿℞ Mercury Retrograde begins (ends April 25)

TUESDAY, APRIL 2

WEDNESDAY, APRIL 3
► Moon void of course begins 1:40 AM EDT
Moon enters Aquarius ♒ 5:08 AM EDT

THURSDAY, APRIL 4

FRIDAY, APRIL 5
► Moon void of course begins 1:39 AM EDT
Moon enters Pisces ♓ 7:13 AM EDT

SATURDAY, APRIL 6

SUNDAY, APRIL 7
► Moon void of course begins 4:27 AM EDT
Moon enters Aries ♈ 7:25 AM EDT

*Work with basil and amethyst
to clear your aura and space.*

APRIL 2024

MONDAY, APRIL 8
☉ Total Solar Eclipse 2:17 PM EDT
New Moon ● ♈ 2:21 PM EDT
► Moon void of course begins 10:39 PM EDT

TUESDAY, APRIL 9
Moon enters Taurus ♉ 7:23 AM EDT

WEDNESDAY, APRIL 10

THURSDAY, APRIL 11
► Moon void of course begins 6:04 AM EDT
Moon enters Gemini ♊ 8:58 AM EDT

FRIDAY, APRIL 12

SATURDAY, APRIL 13
► Moon void of course begins 10:46 AM EDT
Moon enters Cancer ♋ 1:45 AM EDT

SUNDAY, APRIL 14

OWL

*Channel owl energy
to glean wisdom
from a higher
power.*

APRIL 2024

MONDAY, APRIL 15
First Quarter ☽ 3:15 PM EDT
► Moon void of course begins 7:22 PM EDT

TUESDAY, APRIL 16
Moon enters Leo ♌ 10:24 PM EDT

WEDNESDAY, APRIL 17

THURSDAY, APRIL 18
► Moon void of course begins 8:02 AM EDT
Moon enters Virgo ♍ 10:10 AM EDT

FRIDAY, APRIL 19
☉ Sun enters Taurus ♉ 9:59 AM EDT

SATURDAY, APRIL 20
► Moon void of course begins 8:20 PM EDT
Moon enters Virgo ♍ 11:08 PM EDT

SUNDAY, APRIL 21

*To amplify intuitive dreams, place
a sachet of rose petals, amethyst,
and silver under your pillow.*

APRIL 2024

MONDAY, APRIL 22
► Moon void of course begins 7:24 PM EDT

TUESDAY, APRIL 23
Moon enters Scorpio ♏ 11:20 AM EDT
Full Moon ○ ♏ 7:49 PM EDT

WEDNESDAY, APRIL 24

THURSDAY, APRIL 25
► Moon void of course begins 7:17 PM EDT
Moon enters Sagittarius ♐ 9:37 PM EDT
☿℞ Mercury Retrograde ends

FRIDAY, APRIL 26

SATURDAY, APRIL 27

SUNDAY, APRIL 28
► Moon void of course begins 3:31 AM EDT
Moon enters Capricorn ♑ 5:37 AM EDT

*Strengthen your psychic abilities
with horehound tea or mint candy.*

APRIL/MAY 2024

MONDAY, APRIL 29

TUESDAY, APRIL 30
▶ Moon void of course begins 11:19 AM EDT
Moon enters Aquarius ♒ 11:20 AM EDT

WEDNESDAY, MAY 1
★ Beltane (Fixed Festival Date)
Last Quarter ◐ 7:27 AM EDT

Mugwort

THURSDAY, MAY 2
▶ Moon void of course begins 5:28 AM EDT
Moon enters Pisces ♓ 2:52 PM EDT
♇℞ Pluto Retrograde begins (ends Oct. 11)

Elderflowers

FRIDAY, MAY 3

Violets

SATURDAY, MAY 4
★ Beltane (Astronomical Date) 8:11 PM EST
▶ Moon void of course begins 3:06 PM EDT
Moon enters Aries ♈ 4:41 PM EDT

SUNDAY, MAY 5

BELTANE

Feel magical energy growing with your intentions.
Cast flowers into a fire or body of water as you
make a wish for something wonderful.

WITCH'S HAT

Amplify your psychic powers with calendula, cinnamon, or rose.

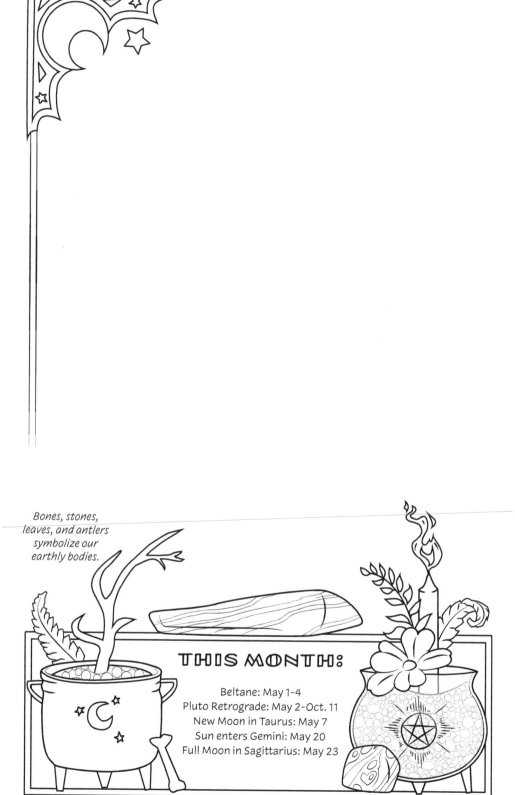

Bones, stones, leaves, and antlers symbolize our earthly bodies.

THIS MONTH:

Beltane: May 1-4
Pluto Retrograde: May 2-Oct. 11
New Moon in Taurus: May 7
Sun enters Gemini: May 20
Full Moon in Sagittarius: May 23

-Earth-
The Element of Stability

Grow plants to feel the magic of the earth.

Ground yourself with smoky quartz.

Grind grains and herbs to connect with their energy.

Place mandrake root with coins to increase abundance.

MAY
POWER OF EARTH
Spend time grounding and aligning with the energy of plants, animals, and nature.
Perform spells to improve your living space.

Wishing Stones have a single unbroken stripe. Make a wish, then bury the stone or throw it into a body of water. Hagstones have holes in them. Nail a hagstone over your door for protection.

Primrose will protect your garden and attract fairies and love.

ELEMENT OF EARTH
ROCK-SOLID SUPPORT FOR YOUR MAGIC

The earth element carries a feeling of belonging, stability, and peace. You "belong" to the Earth as a creature of this planet, and therefore you have a place and purpose. You are capable, secure, meant to be here, and supported in this physical realm.

Earth also represents the cycles of life and death, and the polarity between them—you can't have one without the other.

SIMPLE EARTH SPELLS: The Earth grows new life and also eventually disintegrates it. To use these powers in a spell, bury an herb or a small stone or crystal with the intention of either "to grow" or "to bury" what you wish to let go of. Imagine or feel the energy of what you wish to grow sprouting like a seed, and what you intend to release disintegrating back into the Earth.

Another classic is to plant a seed (or garden) as you set an intention. As you tend to your plant(s), reconnect to your intentions and ground into the energy of what you desire as if it already exists in the physical realm on earth.

CONNECTING WITH EARTH ENERGY:

The simplest way is to just experience nature until you feel your energy shift (you'll know!), or to hold a plant, rock or crystal in your hand and focus on its energy and vibration in your body.

You can also imagine yourself here on Earth, first growing roots, then becoming a giant tree. Grow in your mind's eye until you are viewing the entire planet. Sit with that till your energy shifts, then shrink back into yourself.

And of course, you can use earthy ingredients and energy in any of your spells and rituals.

MAY 2024

	SUNDAY	MONDAY	TUESDAY
	28	29	30
	5	6	7 New Moon ● ♉
	12	13	14
	19	20 ☉ Sun enters Gemini ♊	21
	26	27	28

INTENTIONS
Ground Yourself.

-Mushrooms and Ferns-
The Magic of the Forest

WEDNESDAY	THURSDAY	FRIDAY	SATURDAY
★ Beltane (Fixed Date) 1 Last Quarter ◑	2	3	★ Beltane 8:11 PM EDT 4
8	9	10	11
15 First Quarter ◑	16	17	18
22	23 Full Moon ○ ♐	24	25
29	30 Last Quarter ◑	31	1

MAY 2024

MONDAY, MAY 6
▸ Moon void of course begins 1:57 AM EDT
Moon enters Taurus ♉ 5:42 PM EDT

TUESDAY, MAY 7
New Moon ● ♉ 11:22 PM EDT

WEDNESDAY, MAY 8
▸ Moon void of course begins 5:55 PM EDT
Moon enters Gemini ♊ 7:20 PM EDT

THURSDAY, MAY 9

FRIDAY, MAY 10
▸ Moon void of course begins 9:49 PM EDT
Moon enters Cancer ♋ 11:13 PM EDT

SATURDAY, MAY 11

SUNDAY, MAY 12

*Sweep in the energy of
abundance with a broom made
from wheat straw or vervain.*

MAY 2024

MONDAY, MAY 13
► Moon void of course 5:13 AM EDT
Moon enters Leo ♌ 6:36 AM EDT

TUESDAY, MAY 14

WEDNESDAY, MAY 15
First Quarter ◑ 7:48 AM EDT
► Moon void of course begins 12:41 PM EDT
Moon enters Virgo ♍ 5:33 PM EDT

THURSDAY, MAY 16

FRIDAY, MAY 17

SATURDAY, MAY 18
► Moon void of course begins 5:09 AM EDT
Moon enters Libra ♎ 6:23 AM EDT

SUNDAY, MAY 19
► Moon void of course begins 11:48 AM EDT

BLACKTHORN

*Powerful protection
from dark energy
and calamity.*

MAY 2024

MONDAY, MAY 20
⊙ Sun enters Gemini Ⅱ 8:59 AM EDT
Moon enters Scorpio ♏ 6:34 PM EDT

TUESDAY, MAY 21

WEDNESDAY, MAY 22

THURSDAY, MAY 23
► Moon void of course begins 3:28 AM EDT
Moon enters Sagittarius ♐ 4:24 AM EDT
Full Moon ○ ♐ 9:53 AM EDT

FRIDAY, MAY 24

SATURDAY, MAY 25
► Moon void of course begins 10:47 AM EDT
Moon enters Capricorn ♑ 11:36 AM EDT

SUNDAY, MAY 26

Ground yourself with earthy incense like patchouli, cypress, or vetivert root.

MAY/JUNE 2024

MONDAY, MAY 27
▸ Moon void of course begins 4:02 PM EDT
Moon enters Aquarius ♒ 4:45 PM EDT

TUESDAY, MAY 28

WEDNESDAY, MAY 29
▸ Moon void of course begins 10:20 AM EDT
Moon enters Pisces ♓ 8:33 PM EDT

THURSDAY, MAY 30
Last Quarter ◑ 1:13 PM EDT

FRIDAY, MAY 31
▸ Moon void of course begins 10:55 PM EDT
Moon enters Aries ♈ 11:28 PM EDT

SATURDAY, JUNE 1

SUNDAY, JUNE 2
▸ Moon void of course begins 6:04 PM EDT

GOAT

*Gather your focus
and determination
with goat energy.*

*Spend a few minutes in the sun,
eyes closed, and absorb its power.*

*Work with amber
and amber oil.*

THIS MONTH:

New Moon in Gemini: June 6
Litha (Summer Solstice): June 20
Sun enters Cancer: June 20
Full Moon in Capricorn: June 21
Saturn Retrograde: June 29-Nov. 15

- Fire -
The Element of
Transformation

Make a powerful wand
with rowan wood.

Watch a
candle burn.

- Phoenix -
Rebirth

Anoint your
broom with
cinnamon oil.

Decorate your home or
altar with amaranth.

JUNE
POWER OF FIRE
Transform yourself through letting go
to make space for something new.
Channel the energy of the Phoenix.

Anoint your candles by rubbing a drop or two of essential oil along the length. Then roll your oiled candle in finely crushed herbs.

Fire Burn
AND
Cauldron Bubble

Witch
Hazel

Oak &
Carnelian

Ametrine

ELEMENT OF FIRE
YOUR POWER TO CHANGE AND CREATE

The fire element is a feeling of rapid transformation, contrasting to earth's stable, steady vibe. Fire is the element of movement, passion, action, and change. It also carries an energy of destruction to rebuild and recreate.

SIMPLE FIRE SPELLS: Candles represent fire and the powerful polarity between light and dark. "Charge" your candles with intention—to bring light to a situation, to amplify the energy of your intentions through the fire, or to "burn something out" if you no longer desire it.

Fire is a powerful element for visioning. Gaze into a flame to connect to intuitive messages. Or wrap a bundle of herbs in a piece of paper or natural fabric and burn it with intention.

CONNECTING WITH FIRE ENERGY:
You don't have to use candles to connect to fire! It's all around us. The sun is a big ball of fire, and so are the stars. You can also use the element of fire in cooking or by connecting to the passion and "fire" within yourself.

Try stargazing, ideally until you see a shooting star, then make a wish. You might also like to fire-gaze into a lightning storm or volcano.

Do things that make you feel "heat" in your body, or practice pranayama "Breath of Fire."

Connect to the sun energy by feeling it on your skin (don't stare at it!).

Watch something burn, or destroy something in order to create something new.

Pretend you are a fire-breathing dragon, or imagine you're shooting flaming arrows into the night sky (do not shoot actual flaming arrows without proper precautions and training).

JUNE 2024

	SUNDAY	MONDAY	TUESDAY
	26	27	28
	2	3	4
	9	10	11
	16	17	18
	23	24	25
	30	1	2

INTENTIONS
Destroy to Create

WEDNESDAY	THURSDAY	FRIDAY	SATURDAY
29	30 Last Quarter ◑	31	1
5	6 New Moon ● ♊	7	8
12	13	14 First Quarter ◐	15
19	★ Litha (Summer Solstice) ☉ Sun enters Cancer ♋ 20	21 Full Moon ○ ♐	22
26	27	28 Last Quarter ◑	29
3	4	5 New Moon ● ♋	6

JUNE 2024

MONDAY, JUNE 3
Moon enters Taurus ♉ 1:55 AM EDT

TUESDAY, JUNE 4

WEDNESDAY, JUNE 5
► Moon void of course begins 4:09 AM EDT
Moon enters Gemini ♊ 4:36 AM EDT

THURSDAY, JUNE 6
New Moon ● ♊ 8:38 AM EDT

FRIDAY, JUNE 7
► Moon void of course begins 8:16 AM EDT
Moon enters Cancer ♋ 8:41 AM EDT

SATURDAY, JUNE 8

SUNDAY, JUNE 9
► Moon void of course begins 3:05 PM EDT
Moon enters Leo ♌ 8:41 AM EDT

*Burn rose geranium,
sweet woodruff, or
star anise to connect
with fire energy.*

JUNE 2024

MONDAY, JUNE 10

TUESDAY, JUNE 11
▶ Moon void of course begins 3:16 PM EDT

WEDNESDAY, JUNE 12
Moon enters Virgo ♍ 1:39 AM EDT

THURSDAY, JUNE 13

FRIDAY, JUNE 14
First Quarter ◐ 1:18 AM EDT
▶ Moon void of course begins 1:54 PM EDT
Moon enters Libra ♎ 2:12 PM EDT

SATURDAY, JUNE 15

SUNDAY, JUNE 16

*Feel the energy of
the sun warming
your body.*

JUNE 2024

MONDAY, JUNE 17
▸ Moon void of course begins 2:05 AM EDT
Moon enters Scorpio ♏ 2:38 AM EDT

TUESDAY, JUNE 18

WEDNESDAY, JUNE 19
▸ Moon void of course begins 2:05 AM EDT
Moon enters Sagittarius ♐ 12:32 PM EDT

THURSDAY, JUNE 20
★ Litha (Summer Solstice) 4:51 PM EDT
☉ Sun enters Cancer ♋ 4:51 PM EDT

FRIDAY, JUNE 21
▸ Moon void of course begins 6:58 PM
Moon enters Capricorn ♑ 7:08 PM EDT
Full Moon ○ ♑ 9:08 PM EDT

SATURDAY, JUNE 22

Sweet
Woodruff

SUNDAY, JUNE 23
▸ Moon void of course begins 11:05 PM EDT
Moon enters Aquarius ♒ 11:14 PM EDT

LITHA

*Feel the magic of the sun. Remember that you can
change, grow, and live a bright life by working with
herbs like cinquefoil, woodruff, and cinnamon.*

JUNE 2024

MONDAY, JUNE 24

TUESDAY, JUNE 25
► Moon void of course begins 6:30 PM EDT
Moon enters Pisces ♓ 2:08 AM EDT

WEDNESDAY, JUNE 26

THURSDAY, JUNE 27

FRIDAY, JUNE 28
► Moon void of course begins 4:45 AM EDT
Moon enters Aries ♈ 4:52 AM EDT
Last Quarter ◑ 5:53 PM EDT

SATURDAY, JUNE 29
♄℞ Saturn Retrograde begins (ends November 15)

SUNDAY, JUNE 30
► Moon void of course begins 12:56 AM EDT
Moon enters Taurus ♉ 8:00 AM EDT

Hang St. John's Wort over your door or place it on your altar to bring happiness to your home.

Blue-Green Jade

THIS MONTH:

Neptune Retrograde: July 2–December 7
New Moon in Cancer: July 5
Full Moon in Capricorn: July 21
Sun enters Leo: July 22

*Drink lemon balm tea to evoke
feelings of self-love and success.*

- Water -
The Element of
Emotions

- Aquamarine -
Calming your
thoughts

- Willow -
Moon and
Witch Power

Bathe with eucalyptus to
clarify emotions or with
skullcap for inner peace.

Wash your hair
with jasmine and
rose water.

JULY
POWER OF WATER
Flow with the ups and downs of life as you
follow your intuition and hold your intentions.
Walk along the seashore or near a river or creek.

Make moon water with sea salt, orchids, or lavender to release stagnant
emotional patterns and clear your intuition. Then welcome new energy.

Turquoise

Aloe

Orris Root

FLOW.

Element of Water
The Language of Your Emotions

The water element embodies the power of emotions, intuition, and the wisdom of the subconscious mind. It also represents clearing, washing, releasing, and letting go.

SIMPLE WATER SPELLS: Use the power of water by washing, bathing, or swimming while releasing energy and feeling your intentions.

Try glinting the moon's light off a vessel or a body of water while gazing at its reflection. Or look for shapes that form as the moon dances off the waves or watery ripples.

Classic water spells include blessing yourself in a body of water or tossing herbs or rocks into water while you cast an intention. Pouring or sprinkling water over something to bless it is also a timeless spell, as is making moon waters, baths, floor washes, and blessing waters.

CONNECTING WITH WATER ENERGY:

Submerge yourself in a bath or natural body of water, or pour spring water over your head. Imagine you are the water flowing down a riverbed, or building and releasing in cycles of waves when you face difficult situations.

SOUL BATH: Water is the element of dreams and emotions, and you can use it to listen to the wisdom that exists right now, deep in your soul. Mix 1/2 cup of sea salt and 1/4 cup of dried herbs and petals (like mugwort, jasmine, rose, and lavender). Sprinkle the mix into your bath, or fill a sachet with herbs and tie it under your shower head. Allow yourself to slip into the space between worlds, and ask for the quiet voice of guidance to rise to the surface. Listen closely! Your intuitive voice is subtle and gentle.

JULY 2024

SUNDAY	MONDAY	TUESDAY
30	1	2
7	8	9
14	15	16
21 Full Moon ○ ♑	22 ⊙ Sun enters Leo ♌	23
28	29	30

INTENTIONS
Go with the Flow.

Gardenia & Moonstone

WEDNESDAY	THURSDAY	FRIDAY	SATURDAY
3	4	5 New Moon ● ♋	6
10	11	12	13 First Quarter ◑
17	18	19	20
24	25 ★Lughnasadh (Fixed Date)	26	27 Last Quarter ◑
31	1	2	3

JULY 2024

MONDAY, JULY 1

TUESDAY, JULY 2
► Moon void of course begins 11:43 AM EDT
Moon enters Gemini ♊ 11:50 AM EDT
♆℞ Neptune Retrograde begins (ends December 7)

WEDNESDAY, JULY 3

THURSDAY, JULY 4
► Moon void of course begins 4:44 PM EDT
Moon enters Cancer ♋ 4:51 PM EDT

FRIDAY, JULY 5
New Moon ● ♋ 6:57 PM EDT

SATURDAY, JULY 6
► Moon void of course begins 11:47 PM EDT
Moon enters Leo ♌ 11:56 PM EDT

SUNDAY, JULY 7

Feel calming energies with larimar, valerian root, and chamomile.

JULY 2024

MONDAY, JULY 8

TUESDAY, JULY 9
▸ Moon void of course begins 2:04 AM EDT
Moon enters Virgo ♍ 9:47 AM EDT

WEDNESDAY, JULY 10

THURSDAY, JULY 11
▸ Moon void of course begins 9:55 PM EDT
Moon enters Libra ♎ 10:06 PM EDT

FRIDAY, JULY 12

SATURDAY, JULY 13
▸ Moon void of course begins 6:49 PM EDT
First Quarter ☽ 6:49 PM EDT

SUNDAY, JULY 14
Moon enters Scorpio ♏ 10:53 AM EDT

FROG

Transform in magical ways with frog energy.

JULY 2024

MONDAY, JULY 15

TUESDAY, JULY 16
➤ Moon void of course begins 9:10 PM EDT
Moon enters Sagittarius ♐ 9:25 PM EDT

WEDNESDAY, JULY 17

THURSDAY, JULY 18

FRIDAY, JULY 19
➤ Moon void of course begins 3:58 AM EDT
Moon enters Capricorn ♑ 4:14 AM EDT

SATURDAY, JULY 20

SUNDAY, JULY 21
Full Moon ○ ♑ 6:17 AM EDT
➤ Moon void of course begins 7:26 AM EDT
Moon enters Aquarius ♒ 7:43 AM EDT

Make an elemental floor wash with sprigs of thyme (water), lavender (air), cloves (fire), and vetivert (earth).

JULY 2024

MONDAY, JULY 22
☉ Sun enters Leo ♌ 3:44 AM EDT

TUESDAY, JULY 23
► Moon void of course begins 5:56 AM EDT
Moon enters Pisces ♓ 9:23 AM EDT

WEDNESDAY, JULY 24

THURSDAY, JULY 25
► Moon void of course begins 10:31 AM EDT
Moon enters Aries ♈ 10:52 AM EDT

FRIDAY, JULY 26
► Moon void of course begins 6:14 PM EDT

SATURDAY, JULY 27
Moon enters Taurus ♉ 1:23 PM EDT
Last Quarter ☽ 10:52 PM EDT

SUNDAY, JULY 28

CORNFLOWER

The energy of the moon and changing tides of life.

JULY/AUGUST 2024

MONDAY, JULY 29
► Moon void of course begins 4:59 PM EDT
Moon enters Gemini ♊ 5:28 PM EDT

TUESDAY, JULY 30

WEDNESDAY, JULY 31
► Moon void of course begins 10:46 PM EDT
Moon enters Cancer ♋ 11:19 PM EDT

THURSDAY, AUGUST 1
★ Lughnasadh (Fixed Festival Date)

FRIDAY, AUGUST 2

SATURDAY, AUGUST 3
► Moon void of course begins 6:31 AM EDT
Moon enters Leo ♌ 7:10 AM EDT

SUNDAY, AUGUST 4
New Moon ● ♌ 7:13 AM EDT

LUGHNASADH

Feel the magic of gratitude. Harvest berries or herbs, or bake, eat, and enjoy an abundance of these things in a ritual meal.

- Blackberry -
Protection and Nourishment

Make a wish as you blow the seeds off a dandelion puff.

THIS MONTH:

Lughnasadh: August 1-6
Mercury Retrograde: August 5-28
New Moon in Leo: August 4
Sun enters Virgo: August 22
Full Moon in Aquarius: August 19

- Air -
The Element
of Ideas

Swing a hagstone
on a string to
regain witch
power.

Ring
bells for
protective
magic.

Finding a raven's
feather is a sign of
witch power.

Hang keys or spoons as
wind chimes to stir up or
unlock opportunities.

AUGUST
POWER OF AIR
Use your voice by chanting, singing, playing
music, or expressing yourself through art.
Express thoughts or feelings that've been on your mind.

Watch steam rise off a cup of dandelion tea as you go to sleep. Take a sip of the cold tea in the morning to enhance dream recall and intuitive messages.

AIR ABOVE

Burn acacia wood as you speak your wishes and intentions out loud.

ELEMENT OF AIR
THE MAGIC OF SELF-EXPRESSION AND VOICE

Air symbolizes the power of knowing, in contrast to water's feelings and emotions. Air is the power of your breath and voice (self-expression). Your voice is a powerful force of change and influence in the world, so use it!

The wisdom of air is always flowing through you in your breath. Breath is life, magic, and universal wisdom moving through you at all times.

SIMPLE AIR SPELLS: Air moves energy and magic to you, through you, or away from you, depending on your intention.

Classic "air" spells involve tossing herbs off of a cliff, or tying ribbons to trees that represent wishes, and letting them blow in the breeze. Try casting your spells in a windstorm to increase their energy. You might like to stab the air with a knife (careful, now!) or wildly snip scissors as you speak what you wish to release, such as an energy within yourself or ties with other people.

Use a broom and the power of air to sweep intentions "in" to your door (or clockwise), or sweep "out" (or counterclockwise) to release.

Windows are portals of air's magic. Paint sigils and symbols on your windows, use sun catchers, or place herbs, plants, charms, and crystals on your sills to blow magic inside with the wind.

CONNECTING WITH AIR ENERGY: Find a quiet place to listen to your own breath, or speak things that wish to be spoken, either aloud or through writing or art.

And to receive powerful "air" wisdom, find a good windy spot outdoors and ask the spirit of air to talk to you or provide guidance. Feel and listen closely as the wind blows.

AUGUST 2024

	SUNDAY	MONDAY	TUESDAY
	28	29	30
	4 New Moon ● ♌	5	30 ★ Lughnasadh 8:10 PM EDT 6
	11	12 First Quarter ◐	13
	18	19 Full Moon ○ ♒	20
	25	26 Last Quarter ◐	27

INTENTIONS
Express Yourself.

- Chicory -
Ease

- Blue Lace Agate -
Peaceful Self-Expression

WEDNESDAY	THURSDAY	FRIDAY	SATURDAY
31	★ Lughnasadh (Fixed Date) 1	2	3
7	8	9	10
14	15	16	17
21	☉ Sun enters Virgo ♍ 22	23	24
28	29	30	31

AUGUST 2024

MONDAY, AUGUST 5
► Moon void of course begins 11:16 AM EDT
Moon enters Virgo ♍ 5:17 PM EDT
☿℞ Mercury Retrograde begins (ends August 28)

TUESDAY, AUGUST 6
★ Lughnasadh (Astronomical Date) 8:10 PM EDT

WEDNESDAY, AUGUST 7

THURSDAY, AUGUST 8
► Moon void of course begins 4:40 PM EDT
Moon enters Libra ♎ 5:31 AM EDT

FRIDAY, AUGUST 9
► Moon void of course begins 5:45 PM EDT

SATURDAY, AUGUST 10
Moon enters Scorpio ♏ 6:34 PM EDT

SUNDAY, AUGUST 11

*If you find a raven's feather,
wear it in your hat for energetic
protection and witch power.*

AUGUST 2024

MONDAY, AUGUST 12
First Quarter ◑ 11:19 AM EDT

TUESDAY, AUGUST 13
► Moon void of course begins 5:01 AM EDT
Moon enters Sagittarius ♐ 6:01 AM EDT

WEDNESDAY, AUGUST 14

THURSDAY, AUGUST 15
► Moon void of course begins 12:52 PM EDT
Moon enters Capricorn ♑ 1:51 PM EDT

FRIDAY, AUGUST 16

SATURDAY, AUGUST 17
► Moon void of course begins 4:43 PM EDT
Moon enters Aquarius ♒ 5:45 PM EDT

SUNDAY, AUGUST 18

RAVEN

*Channel raven
energy to speak
from your heart.*

AUGUST 2024

MONDAY, AUGUST 19
► Moon void of course begins 2:26 PM EDT
Full Moon ○ ≈ 2:26 PM EDT
Moon enters Pisces ♓ 6:52 PM EDT

TUESDAY, AUGUST 20

WEDNESDAY, AUGUST 21
► Moon void of course begins 5:54 PM EDT
Moon enters Aries ♈ 7:02 PM EDT

THURSDAY, AUGUST 22
☉ Sun enters Virgo ♍ 10:54 AM EDT

FRIDAY, AUGUST 23
► Moon void of course begins 8:44 AM EDT
Moon enters Taurus ♉ 8:00 PM EDT

SATURDAY, AUGUST 24

SUNDAY, AUGUST 25
► Moon void of course begins 9:40 PM EDT
Moon enters Gemini ♊ 11:04 PM EDT

*Plant a window box with herbs that signify
your intentions. Open the window and let
the breeze blow magic into your house.*

AUGUST/SEPTEMBER 2024

MONDAY, AUGUST 26
Last Quarter ☽ 5:26 AM EDT

TUESDAY, AUGUST 27

WEDNESDAY, AUGUST 28
▸ Moon void of course begins 3:14 AM EDT
Moon enters Cancer ♋ 4:47 AM EDT
☿℞ Mercury Retrograde ends

THURSDAY, AUGUST 29

FRIDAY, AUGUST 30
▸ Moon void of course begins 11:24 AM EDT
Moon enters Leo ♌ 1:09 AM EDT

SATURDAY, AUGUST 31

SUNDAY, SEPTEMBER 1
▸ Moon void of course begins 8:25 PM EDT
Moon enters Virgo ♍ 11:48 PM EDT
♅℞ Uranus Retrograde begins (ends Jan. 30, 2025)

SCISSORS

Cut fresh herbs (like mint) to help you make decisions.

THIS MONTH:

Uranus Retrograde: September 1 -Jan. 30, 2025
New Moon in Virgo: September 2
Full Moon in Pisces: September 17
Partial Lunar Eclipse: September 17
Sun enters Libra: September 22
Mabon (Autumnal Equinox): September 22

- Pentacle -
The Laws of Magic

-Herkimer
Diamond-
Attuning
to Spirit

Fly beyond your
limitations.

Consecrate your robe &
hat with magical scents.

Follow your curiosity &
desires of your spirit.

SEPTEMBER
POWER OF SPIRIT
Reconnect to the experiences, rituals, and everyday
things that make you feel magical.
Listen closely to your intuition and follow it.

YOU ARE THE SPELL.

WEAVING THE WEB
CREATE YOUR SIGNATURE SPELL

By now you're familiar with the magic of the four elements (earth, fire, air, and water). Many witches believe that the fifth point of the pentagram represents the fifth element—SPIRIT.

So how do you connect with spirit or perform a spell of spirit?! This is personal and unique to you. Spirit is the magic that only you can do, and you don't need a written spell to do it.

WHAT IS SACRED TO YOU? What scents, sights, sounds, and mechanisms evoke magic within you? Is it all within your mind and energetic body? Or do you use herbs, candles, or representations of the four physical elements? Give it a feel and then write it down. There is no right and wrong here. Just search for the things that make you *feel the magic* within.

You might like to pick one tool that you keep constant throughout your work (like a cauldron, wand, crystal, figurine, broom, hat, or robe).

It's also helpful to pick one signature scent (an incense or oil) that you use only for magic, so when you smell it, you'll be automatically moved to the feeling of spirit and magic within.

CREATE YOUR SIGNATURE SPELL: This will be a spell that you know intuitively, so you can do it anytime for any intention. It can be simple, but that's up to you. Use this example as a starting point or create something entirely unique.

Carve your name, a deity's name, or a symbol into a candle. Light the candle and a cauldron of incense. Cast a circle, moving until you feel your energy shift. Sit in the circle. Chant until you feel a tingly sense of magic within. Speak your intention, then listen for intuitive wisdom.

SEPTEMBER 2024

	SUNDAY	MONDAY	TUESDAY
	1	2 New Moon ● ♍	3
	8	9	10 ★Partial Lunar Eclipse
	15	16	17 Full Moon ○ ♓
	22 ☉ Sun enters Libra ♎ ★Mabon (Autumnal Equinox)	23	24 Last Quarter ◑
	29	30	1

INTENTIONS
Stay True to Yourself.

- Zoisite -
*Living as Your
Authentic Self*

- Olive -
Purity of Spirit

WEDNESDAY	THURSDAY	FRIDAY	SATURDAY
4	5	6	7
11 First Quarter ◑	12	13	14
18	19	20	21
25	26	27	28
2 New Moon ● ♎	3	4	5

SEPTEMBER 2024

MONDAY, SEPTEMBER 2
New Moon ● ♍ 9:56 PM EDT

TUESDAY, SEPTEMBER 3

WEDNESDAY, SEPTEMBER 4
► Moon void of course begins 12:06 PM EDT
Moon enters Libra ♎ 12:12 PM EDT

THURSDAY, SEPTEMBER 5

FRIDAY, SEPTEMBER 6

SATURDAY, SEPTEMBER 7
► Moon void of course begins 1:08 AM EDT
Moon enters Scorpio ♏ 1:18 AM EDT

SUNDAY, SEPTEMBER 8

*Use your favorite sacred herb or incense in
your rituals to associate that scent with
magic and amplify its suggestive power.*

SEPTEMBER 2024

MONDAY, SEPTEMBER 9
► Moon void of course begins 1:11 PM EDT
Moon enters Sagittarius ♐ 1:26 PM EDT

TUESDAY, SEPTEMBER 10

WEDNESDAY, SEPTEMBER 11
First Quarter ◑ 2:06 AM EDT
► Moon void of course begins 8:21 PM EDT
Moon enters Capricorn ♑ 10:38 PM EDT

THURSDAY, SEPTEMBER 12

FRIDAY, SEPTEMBER 13

SATURDAY, SEPTEMBER 14
► Moon void of course begins 3:35 AM EDT
Moon enters Aquarius ♒ 3:53 AM EDT

SUNDAY, SEPTEMBER 15

THE VEIL

What does "spirit" mean to you? When do you feel spiritual?

SEPTEMBER 2024

MONDAY, SEPTEMBER 16
► Moon void of course begins 1:04 AM EDT
Moon enters Pisces ♓ 5:39 AM EDT

TUESDAY, SEPTEMBER 17
Full Moon ○ ♓ 10:34 PM EDT
Partial Lunar Eclipse 10:44 PM EDT

WEDNESDAY, SEPTEMBER 18
► Moon void of course begins 5:02 AM EDT
Moon enters Aries ♈ 5:24 AM EDT

THURSDAY, SEPTEMBER 19

FRIDAY, SEPTEMBER 20
► Moon void of course begins 4:39 AM EDT
Moon enters Taurus ♉ 5:03 AM EDT

SATURDAY, SEPTEMBER 21

SUNDAY, SEPTEMBER 22
☉ Sun enters Libra ♎ 8:43 AM EDT
★ Mabon (Autumnal Equinox) 8:43 AM EDT

MABON

*Feel the magic of release. Courageously follow
your intuition towards what you desire, and
allow yourself to slowly let go of the rest.*

SEPTEMBER 2024

MONDAY, SEPTEMBER 23

TUESDAY, SEPTEMBER 24
► Moon void of course begins 7:59 AM EDT
Moon enters Cancer ♋ 10:50 AM EDT
Last Quarter ◑ 2:50 PM EST

WEDNESDAY, SEPTEMBER 25

THURSDAY, SEPTEMBER 26
► Moon void of course begins 6:12 PM EDT
Moon enters Leo ♌ 6:47 PM EDT

FRIDAY, SEPTEMBER 27

SATURDAY, SEPTEMBER 28
► Moon void of course begins 11:36 PM EDT

SUNDAY, SEPTEMBER 29
Moon enters Virgo ♍ 5:42 AM EDT

*Burn apple wood or enjoy the
taste of apples to remind you
of the immortality of spirit.*

SEPTEMBER/OCTOBER 2024

MONDAY, SEPTEMBER 30

TUESDAY, OCTOBER 1
► Moon void of course begins 5:39 PM EDT
Moon enters Libra ♎ 6:20 PM EDT

WEDNESDAY, OCTOBER 2
New Moon ● ♎ 2:49 PM EDT
Annular Solar Eclipse 2:44 PM EDT

THURSDAY, OCTOBER 3

FRIDAY, OCTOBER 4
► Moon void of course begins 6:40 AM EDT
Moon enters Scorpio ♏ 7:22 AM EDT

SATURDAY, OCTOBER 5

SUNDAY, OCTOBER 6
► Moon void of course begins 10:52 AM EDT
Moon enters Sagittarius ♐ 7:34 PM EDT

- Kyanite & Clary Sage -
Connection to Spirit Guides

FLIGHT

*Trust yourself and
follow your spirit.*

Place statues of toads or gargoyles to protect your home and garden.

THIS MONTH:

New Moon in Libra: October 2
Annular Solar Eclipse: October 2
Jupiter ℞: Oct. 9-Feb. 4, 2025
Pluto ℞ ends: October 11
Full Moon in Aries: October 17
Sun enters Scorpio: October 22
Samhain: Oct. 31- Nov. 6

Interlocking patterns are protective.

- Magic Knot -
Elemental Protection

Yarrow

Nails signify protection.

- Witch Bottles -
A classic!

Burdock Root

White candles protect your magic.

Enchant a lock and key.

Set protective charms at doors, windows, & thresholds.

OCTOBER
PROTECTION
Create a sacred space where you feel safe, secure, and surrounded by your magic.
Cast a perimeter spell around your home.

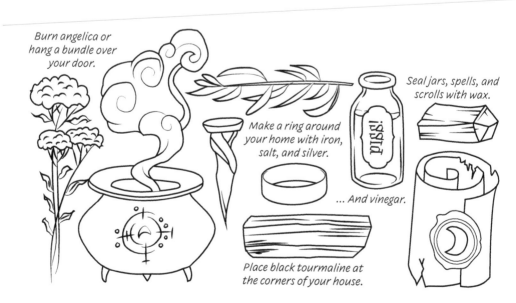

Burn angelica or hang a bundle over your door.

Make a ring around your home with iron, salt, and silver.

Seal jars, spells, and scrolls with wax.

Piss!

... And vinegar.

Place black tourmaline at the corners of your house.

IN THIS CIRCLE...

Place bay leaves at the four corners of your home.

Design your own protection sigil and draw it in this shield.

NO HARM SHALL PASS.

PROTECTION SPELLS
CREATE AN ENERGETIC SHIELD

A shield or protection spell is an energetic boundary. Shields create a magical space where you decide what may enter, and what may not.

The purpose of "casting a circle" in spellcraft is to create a container for your magic spell and also to form a protective shield. Circles, interlocking shapes, and symbols made of unbroken lines (like the pentagram) are ancient mechanisms of energetic protection.

PROTECTION AND SHIELDING SPELLS:

The "classic" energetic shield involves creating a bubble of light or an "egg" around you where no harm shall pass. Imagine the "vibes" and things you do not wish to reach you bouncing off the outside of the shield. Decide what your boundaries are and adhere to them. You might like to refresh your shield each day.

If you do run into an energy outside of your boundary, (events, conversations, trains of thought, etc.) try your best to not engage. Put up your shield and re-set that energetic line.

There are endless ways to use physical magic and amulets for protection, too. Charge a piece of jewelry, crystal, or amulet that you carry with you. Or create a charm to hang in your home— a pentacle over your door, salt sprinkled at the four corners, or a bundle of herbs will help to dissipate or "send back" whatever energy you do not wish to enter your space.

You might try placing statues or symbols of gargoyles, dragons, or other fierce creatures and charge them with your protective intentions.

And carry an aura of confidence and power with you wherever you go. You are a witch!

OCTOBER 2024

SUNDAY	MONDAY	TUESDAY
29	30	1
6	7	8
13	14	15
20	21	22 ⊙ Sun enters Scorpio
27	28	29

Jet & Onyx

INTENTIONS
Protect Your Energy.

Heather, Bay, & Rosemary

WEDNESDAY	THURSDAY	FRIDAY	SATURDAY
★ Annular Solar Eclipse 2 New Moon ● ♎	3	4	5
9	10 First Quarter ◗	11	12
16	17 Full Moon ○ ♈	18	19
23	24 Last Quarter ◖ ★ Samhain (fixed date)	25	26
30	31	1 New Moon ● ♏	2

OCTOBER 2024

MONDAY, OCTOBER 7

TUESDAY, OCTOBER 8

WEDNESDAY, OCTOBER 9
► Moon void of course begins 1:54 AM EDT
Moon enters Capricorn ♑ 5:38 AM EDT
♃℞ Jupiter Retrograde begins (ends Feb. 4, 2025)

THURSDAY, OCTOBER 10
First Quarter ☽ 2:55 PM EDT

FRIDAY, OCTOBER 11
► Moon void of course begins 11:53 AM EDT
Moon enters Aquarius ♒ 12:31 PM EDT
♇℞ Pluto Retrograde ends

SATURDAY, OCTOBER 12

SUNDAY, OCTOBER 13
► Moon void of course begins 10:11 AM EDT
Moon enters Pisces ♓ 3:55 PM EDT

Anoint candles or burn an oil lamp with olive oil and a few drops of cypress oil.

OCTOBER 2024

MONDAY, OCTOBER 14

TUESDAY, OCTOBER 15
► Moon void of course begins 4:00 PM EDT
Moon enters Aries ♈ 4:34 PM EDT

WEDNESDAY, OCTOBER 16

THURSDAY, OCTOBER 17
Full Moon ○ ♈ 7:26 AM EDT
► Moon void of course begins 3:26 PM EDT
Moon enters Taurus ♉ 4:00 PM EDT

FRIDAY, OCTOBER 18

SATURDAY, OCTOBER 19
► Moon void of course begins 3:33 PM EDT
Moon enters Gemini ♊ 4:07 PM EDT

SUNDAY, OCTOBER 20

MULLEIN

Sprinkle mullein around your house.

OCTOBER 2024

MONDAY, OCTOBER 21
▸ Moon void of course begins 5:00 PM EDT
Moon enters Cancer ♋ 6:50 PM EDT

TUESDAY, OCTOBER 22
☉ Sun enters Scorpio ♏ 6:14 PM EDT

WEDNESDAY, OCTOBER 23

THURSDAY, OCTOBER 24
▸ Moon void of course begins 12:47 AM EDT
Moon enters Leo ♌ 1:24 AM EDT
Last Quarter ◑ 4:03 AM EST

FRIDAY, OCTOBER 25

*Scary faces on
Jack-o-Lanterns
will protect you!*

SATURDAY, OCTOBER 26
▸ Moon void of course begins 4:04 AM EDT
Moon enters Virgo ♍ 11:47AM EDT

SUNDAY, OCTOBER 27

SAMHAIN

*Feel the possibilities and magic in the darkness.
Create a charm bag with iron, salt, and silver to
protect your spirit as you venture into the unknown.*

MONDAY, OCTOBER 28
➤ Moon void of course begins 11:54 PM EDT

TUESDAY, OCTOBER 29
Moon enters Libra ♎ 12:30 AM EDT

WEDNESDAY, OCTOBER 30

THURSDAY, OCTOBER 31
★ Samhain (Fixed Festival Date)
➤ Moon void of course begins 12:57 PM EDT
Moon enters Scorpio ♏ 1:29 PM EDT

FRIDAY, NOVEMBER 1
New Moon ● ♏ 8:47 AM EDT

SATURDAY, NOVEMBER 2

*Make a kitchen witch's
protection charm with parsley,
dill, fennel, or rosemary. Tie the
herbs with a black or red string.*

SUNDAY, NOVEMBER 3
➤ Moon void of course begins 12:51 AM EDT
Moon enters Sagittarius ♐ 1:19 AM EDT

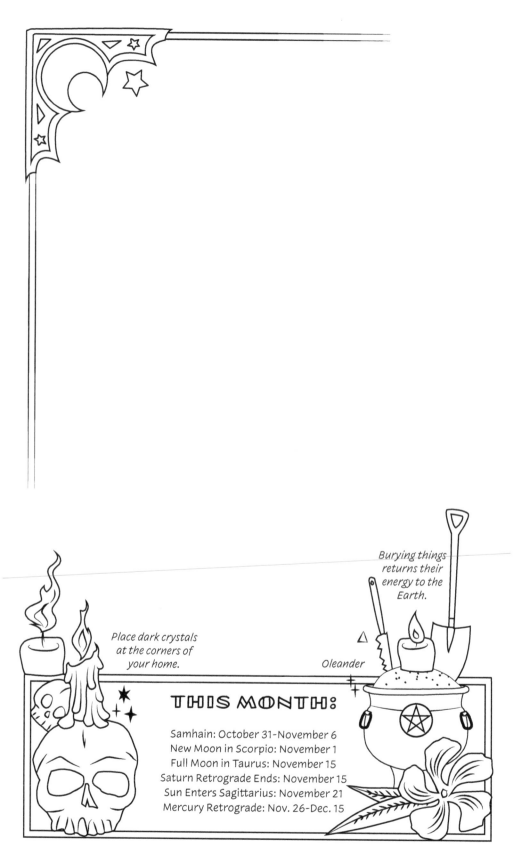

Place dark crystals at the corners of your home.

Oleander

Burying things returns their energy to the Earth.

THIS MONTH:

Samhain: October 31-November 6
New Moon in Scorpio: November 1
Full Moon in Taurus: November 15
Saturn Retrograde Ends: November 15
Sun Enters Sagittarius: November 21
Mercury Retrograde: Nov. 26-Dec. 15

Scorpio

Sagittarius

- Mystic Star -
Power of the Witch

Bats and
dark creatures
signify the magic of
the unknown.

Heliotrope

Burning
releases
energy.

Anoint knives
& scissors
with clove oil.

Four Thieves Vinegar

Belladonna

NOVEMBER
BANISHING
Decide what no longer serves your life,
magic, and intentions. Then banish them.
Clear out your physical and mental spaces.

What will set you free?

BANISHING & RELEASE
THE MOST POWERFUL SPELLS OF ALL

Banishing spells are a witch's classic! You might want to banish a thought, a pattern, a habit, or a person. However, you're actually banishing emotions and energy within yourself.

Part of banishing is surrender. This doesn't mean "to give up," but to accept what's happened. Then you can banish what you no longer desire with one of these delightful spells.

CLASSIC BANISHING: Burn things! Burning a piece of paper with written intentions or herbs with an energetic charge is simple and effective.

Or tie a natural fiber around two candles, then burn the candles until the cord breaks. You can also cut a cord or string with scissors or a sword, or imagine it in your mind's eye.

The toilet paper spell?! Yep. Write what you wish to banish on toilet paper and then flush it.

Burying things with intention (like natural paper, herbs, or rocks) will neutralize energy.

Baths and showers are also effective to release and wash energy down the drain.

Broom spells can also help to get the job done. Try sweeping energy out your front door.

For any of these spells, practice shifting your attention. First, feel and say all of your feelings. Like, "I feel ___ (disappointed, full of woe, etc.) but I intend to banish that now." Then practice shifting your attention towards what you desire.

The most effective banishing spell of all is to no longer give "it" your attention. Attention and intention are powerful magic. You might need to repeat this shift multiple times. Eventually you'll realize the energy has left your life, and you have completed a successful banishing spell.

NOVEMBER 2024

	SUNDAY	MONDAY	TUESDAY
	27	28	29
	3	4	5
	10	11	12
	17	18	19
	24	25	26

INTENTIONS
Release Your Past.

Hellebore

WEDNESDAY	THURSDAY	FRIDAY	SATURDAY
30	★ Samhain (fixed date) 31	1 New Moon ● ♏	2
★ Samhain 5:21 PM 6	7	8	9 First Quarter ◐
13	14	15 Full Moon ○ ♉	16
20	⊙ Sun Enters Sagittarius 21	22 Last Quarter ◑	23
27	28	29	30

NOVEMBER 2024

MONDAY, NOVEMBER 4

TUESDAY, NOVEMBER 5
▶ Moon void of course begins 5:23 AM EST
Moon enters Capricorn ♑ 10:17 AM EST

WEDNESDAY, NOVEMBER 6
★ Samhain (Astronomical Date) 5:21 PM EST

THURSDAY, NOVEMBER 7
▶ Moon void of course begins 5:38 PM EST
Moon enters Aquarius ♒ 5:58 PM EST

FRIDAY, NOVEMBER 8

SATURDAY, NOVEMBER 9
First Quarter ◑ 12:55 AM EST
▶ Moon void of course begins 7:23 PM EST
Moon enters Pisces ♓ 11:00 PM EST

SUNDAY, NOVEMBER 10

*Cast agrimony, hyssop, vetivert, or
rowan into a fire to release the past.*

NOVEMBER 2024

MONDAY, NOVEMBER 11
► Moon void of course begins 1:13 AM EST
Moon enters Aries ♈ 1:26 AM EST

TUESDAY, NOVEMBER 12

WEDNESDAY, NOVEMBER 13

THURSDAY, NOVEMBER 14
► Moon void of course begins 1:50 AM EST
Moon enters Taurus ♉ 1:59 AM EST

FRIDAY, NOVEMBER 15
Full Moon ○ ♉ 4:29 PM EST
♄℞ Saturn Retrograde ends

SATURDAY, NOVEMBER 16
► Moon void of course begins 2:03 AM EST
Moon enters Gemini ♊ 2:09 AM EST

SUNDAY, NOVEMBER 17
► Moon void of course begins 11:09 PM EST

Sweep counterclockwise to release and clear energy.

NOVEMBER 2024

MONDAY, NOVEMBER 18
Moon enters Cancer ♋ 3:50 AM EST

TUESDAY, NOVEMBER 19

WEDNESDAY, NOVEMBER 20
▶ Moon void of course begins 6:20 AM EST
Moon enters Leo ♌ 8:51 AM EST

THURSDAY, NOVEMBER 21
☉ Sun enters Sagittarius ♐ 2:56 PM EST

FRIDAY, NOVEMBER 22
▶ Moon void of course begins 8:15 AM EST
Moon enters Virgo ♍ 6:01 PM EST
Last Quarter ◑ 8:28 PM EST

SATURDAY, NOVEMBER 23

SUNDAY, NOVEMBER 24

To make a banishing water, mix a drop of lavender oil with spring water and salt, and leave it out under the waning moon.

NOVEMBER/DECEMBER 2024

MONDAY, NOVEMBER 25
► Moon void of course begins 12:35 AM EST
Moon enters Libra ♎ 6:20 AM EST

TUESDAY, NOVEMBER 26
☿℞ Mercury Retrograde begins (ends Dec. 15)

WEDNESDAY, NOVEMBER 27
► Moon void of course begins 4:14 AM EST

THURSDAY, NOVEMBER 28
Moon enters Scorpio ♏ 7:21 PM EST

FRIDAY, NOVEMBER 29

SATURDAY, NOVEMBER 30
► Moon void of course begins 1:19 AM EST
Moon enters Sagittarius ♐ 6:53 AM EST

SUNDAY, DECEMBER 1
New Moon ● ♐ 1:21 AM EST

DRAGON

Use the symbolism of dragons to banish things.

THIS MONTH:

New Moon in Sagittarius: December 1
Mars Retrograde: December 6-Feb. 23, 2025
Neptune Retrograde ends: December 7
Full Moon in Gemini: December 15
Mercury Retrograde ends: December 15
Yule (Winter Solstice): December 21
Sun enters Capricorn: December 21
New (Black) Moon in Capricorn: Dec. 30

Twelve Pointed Star
Universal Energy

Sovereignty

"Only asphodels can grow
in the meadow of the soul."

- Anima Mundi -
The Soul of the World

DECEMBER
POWER OF ENERGY
Look at patterns in your life to identify
who you are in the totality of your soul.
Ask to know and follow your soul's purpose.

Roses emit the
highest frequency
of any flower.

Smell a rose to
raise your energetic
vibration.

SPIRITUAL EVOLUTION
MAGIC FOR YOUR SOUL

You don't "have" a soul; you are a soul.

Spells often carry the intention of a specific purpose, usually to gain or release something.

But there is distinct kind of magic beyond that: magic with the intention of raising consciousness or evolving on a spiritual, energetic, divine, or "soul" level. Some call it "high magic." It's also known as "The Great Work" in alchemy.

It's not as lofty as it sounds because your soul (or the divine) wants to teach you about itself.

If you ask for the mystical to reveal itself—if you intend to experience it—you will find it.

RITUALS FOR SPIRITUAL EVOLUTION:

Consciousness exists through us, experiencing it through ourselves, so anything that evokes a tingling of your spine can create transcendence. Ceremonial magic is a classic method, as

performing a ritual heightens your reality.

Meditation is also extremely effective, as is chanting, humming, breath work, sacred movement (dance, yoga, kundalini)—anything that puts you in a trance-like state. Or you might prefer to work with sacred geometry or art.

So, what works for you? Experiment until you find it. Then perform that "spell" until you feel the energy rise up your spine and body. When you reach that feeling, imagine yourself surrounded by radiant, pure light. Feel this light permeating and buzzing within every cell of your being, till you feel your energy shift. Give it time and patience. You will feel it. That's the energy of the soul, and that's your magic. Put out your hands, accept that magic, and use it well. You are a soul, and you are magic incarnate.

DECEMBER 2024

	SUNDAY	MONDAY	TUESDAY
	1 New Moon ● ♐	2	3
	8 First Quarter ◗	9	10
	15 Full Moon ○ ♊	16	17
	22 Last Quarter ◖	23	24
	29	30 New Moon ● ♑	31

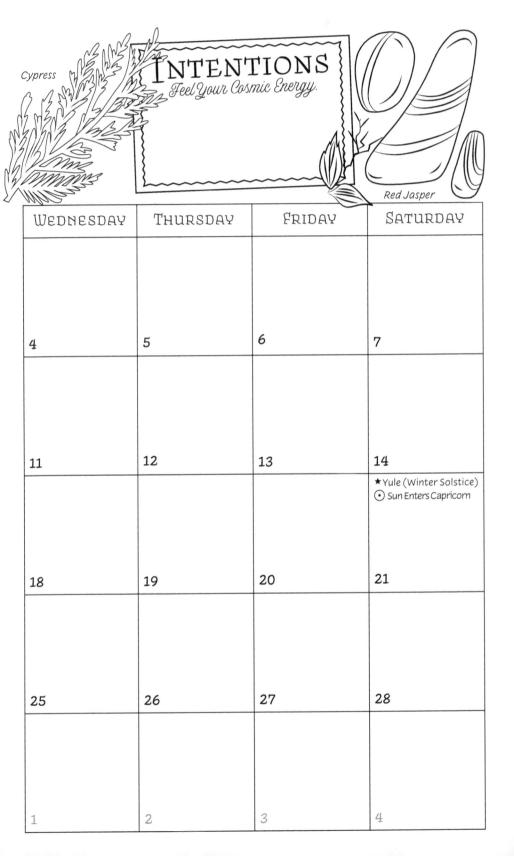

Cypress

INTENTIONS
Feel Your Cosmic Energy.

Red Jasper

WEDNESDAY	THURSDAY	FRIDAY	SATURDAY
4	5	6	7
11	12	13	14
18	19	20	21 ★ Yule (Winter Solstice) ☉ Sun Enters Capricorn
25	26	27	28
1	2	3	4

DECEMBER 2024

MONDAY, DECEMBER 2
▸ Moon void of course begins 10:47 AM EST
Moon enters Capricorn ♑ 4:09 PM EST

TUESDAY, DECEMBER 3

WEDNESDAY, DECEMBER 4
▸ Moon void of course begins 6:34 PM EST
Moon enters Aquarius ♒ 11:21 PM EST

THURSDAY, DECEMBER 5

FRIDAY, DECEMBER 6
▸ Moon void of course begins 7:01 PM EST
♂℞ Mars Retrograde begins (ends Feb. 23, 2025)

SATURDAY, DECEMBER 7
Moon enters Pisces ♓ 4:49 AM EST
♆℞ Neptune Retrograde ends

SUNDAY, DECEMBER 8
First Quarter ☽ 10:27 AM EST

Work with bloodstone and holly to feel peace in the present moment.

DECEMBER 2024

MONDAY, DECEMBER 9
► Moon void of course begins 3:45 AM EST
Moon enters Aries ♈ 8:38 AM EST

TUESDAY, DECEMBER 10
► Moon void of course begins 5:13 PM EST

WEDNESDAY, DECEMBER 11
Moon enters Taurus ♉ 10:55 AM EST

THURSDAY, DECEMBER 12

FRIDAY, DECEMBER 13
► Moon void of course begins 7:39 AM EST
Moon enters Gemini ♊ 12:22 PM EST

SATURDAY, DECEMBER 14

SUNDAY, DECEMBER 15
Full Moon ○ ♊ 4:02 AM EST
► Moon void of course begins 9:32 AM EST
Moon enters Cancer ♋ 2:21 PM EST
☿℞ Mercury Retrograde ends

YEW

Yew makes an powerful wand, but handle with care. It's toxic!

DECEMBER 2024

MONDAY, DECEMBER 16

TUESDAY, DECEMBER 17
► Moon void of course begins 1:33 AM EST
Moon enters Leo ♌ 2:21 AM EST

WEDNESDAY, DECEMBER 18

THURSDAY, DECEMBER 19

FRIDAY, DECEMBER 20
► Moon void of course begins 12:19 AM EST
Moon enters Virgo ♍ 2:37 AM EST

SATURDAY, DECEMBER 21
★ Yule (Winter Solstice) 4:21 AM EST
☉ Sun enters Capricorn ♑ 4:21 AM EST

SUNDAY, DECEMBER 22
► Moon void of course begins 8:27 AM EST
Moon enters Libra ♎ 12:08 PM EST
Last Quarter ☽ 5:17 PM EST

YULE

Feel the magic of peace and acceptance. Decorate your home with herbs and evergreens to bring light and energy to yourself in the present.

DECEMBER 2024

MONDAY, DECEMBER 23

TUESDAY, DECEMBER 24
▶ Moon void of course begins 5:44 AM EST
Moon enters Scorpio ♏ 3:06 AM EST

WEDNESDAY, DECEMBER 25

THURSDAY, DECEMBER 26

FRIDAY, DECEMBER 27
▶ Moon void of course begins 9:24 AM EST
Moon enters Sagittarius ♐ 2:46 AM EST

*Ivy and evergreens
symbolize the
immortality of the soul.*

SATURDAY, DECEMBER 28

SUNDAY, DECEMBER 29
▶ Moon void of course begins 6:34 PM EST
Moon enters Capricorn ♑ 11:37 PM EST

DECEMBER 2024/JANUARY 2025

MONDAY, DECEMBER 30
New (Black) Moon ● ♑ 5:27 PM EST

TUESDAY, DECEMBER 31

WEDNESDAY, JANUARY 1, 2025
► Moon void of course begins 1:02 AM EST
Moon enters Aquarius ♒ 5:50 AM EST

THURSDAY, JANUARY 2, 2025
► Moon void of course begins 11:13 PM EST

FRIDAY, JANUARY 3, 2025
Moon enters Pisces ♓ 10:21 AM EST

SATURDAY, JANUARY 4, 2025

SUNDAY, JANUARY 5, 2025
► Moon void of course begins 9:30 AM EST
Moon enters Aries ♈ 2:01 PM EST

Open your doors and windows and sweep out the energy of the old year to ring in the new.

Congratulations!
13
WITCH POWERS
ACTIVATED!

How will you use these powers?
What's next for you?!

Wendy Ledger
Editor
WendyLedgerAuthor.com

Bollank
Art Production

Fiona Horne
Editor of Magick
& Editor
FionaHorne.com

Kae Marie Denino
Editor

THANK YOU!

About the Artist

Amy Cesari
(and her familiar, Cornelius)

Amy is an author and illustrator who loves animated musicals. She also likes watercolor painting, witchcraft, and walking on the beach in a really big sun hat.

Not only does she own every Nintendo game console ever made, she's earned several fancy diplomas and enjoys continued studies in various magical practices.

CONTACT AMY AND SEE MORE BOOKS, PRINTABLE PAGES, AND ART:

Amy@ColoringBookofShadows.com
ColoringBookofShadows.com

Printed in the USA
CPSIA information can be obtained
at www.ICGtesting.com
LVHW072031241023
762003LV00001B/2

Coloring Book of Shadows

Planner for A Magical

2024

Amy Cesari

Be a fire-safe witch!

Lots of space above and around the flame.

Candle is on a fire-safe dish.

Never leave flames unattended.

- Thirteen Powers -

This book will take you through twelve spells to "unlock" or show you
the depths of your witch powers. You've already got the most important
(the thirteenth...) so go ahead and check that off below. *Check!*

13
THE POWER
OF YOU

You've already
got this!
☐

| **01** DESIRE Claim what you want. ☐ | **02** SHADOW Find what you've hidden. ☐ | **03** INTENTION Take action & believe. ☐ | **04** THE MIND Follow your intuition. ☐ | **05** EARTH Feel that you belong. ☐ | **06** FIRE Know that you can change. ☐ |

- Unlock Them All! -

As you do each spell in the book and "feel" the power it describes, check off the boxes below. At the end of the year (or sooner if you're an overachiever!), you'll find you've activated your full witch power.

07
WATER
Feel your
emotions.
☐

08
AIR
Know what
you think.
☐

09
SPIRIT
Know your
soul's magic.
☐

10
PROTECTION
Create
your space.
☐

11
BANISHING
Release & let
things go.
☐

12
ENERGY
Know you're
limitless.
☐

Hail and Welcome to Your Magical 2024

MAGIC?! YOU'VE GOT THIS.

The most widely accepted definition of magic is the ability to influence your destiny. To align your intention, will, and the natural forces around you—such as the moon, the sun, the planets, and the changing seasons—is magic.

Magic is like an invisible thread. You may barely notice it's there at times. But if you hang onto that thread of intention (and action) through the many moons and phases of your year, that magic will come through for you in life-changing ways.

This book isn't about planning to do more, but about prioritizing magic in your life and pulling that thread forward, amidst the ups and downs.

You've already got what you need to make this year magical. Are you ready? *Say yes!*

YOU'RE CAPABLE AND READY FOR IT.

You may already be familiar with the 12 "witch powers" in this book. If you are, that's great news, because it means you're ready to strengthen your connection to magic as you work through these spells, and unlock new levels of witch power.

If these powers are new to you, you'll likely feel a hint of recognition as you do the work, as if you're remembering a "lost" magic from your past. And if not? If magic feels new to you, cherish these first emerging moments of your powers—they are potent.

So are you ready to feel that magic?! Rub your hands together till you feel energy move down your arms, to your spine, and through your body. Then hold your palms out and say, "The magic is mine!" (and cackle maniacally if you wish!).

You'll feel that spark, because your "witch powers" are already within you, just waiting to be activated. So consider this your invitation and permission slip to believe in the power of you... and your capacity to make real magic happen.

Believing in your magic means knowing that you are capable. You've plunged into darkness many times before, and you've weathered a few storms... yes? Knowing that, you can believe in yourself and believe in your magic to make things happen.

So, say yes to what you desire, to what you wish to change, and to the magic of the dark, the light, and everything in-between. Your witch powers are always there for you, and they will help you navigate your journey through life.

Wield Thy Power!
THE MAGIC
Is Yours.

TIPS TO USE THIS PLANNER

1. Familiarize yourself with the introduction and basics of magic and spellcasting.
2. Fill out the "MAGICAL VISION" planning pages at the end of the introduction.
3. Try to perform the "big spell" or one of the mini-spells in this book each month.
4. Review your MAGICAL VISION monthly, whenever you like, or on the new moon. Adjust as needed, then break your goals into smaller intentions and actions for the month, and try to keep moving forward. Step by step.
5. Repeat this process for as many of the 12 months of the year as you can to "stir the cauldron"... and see what happens. (It'll be magic!)

• There is only one rule: you're not allowed to stress about "keeping up" on coloring the whole book. Enjoy the parts you do color *if any*, and don't worry about the rest.
• Since this book is printed on both sides of the page, it works best if you use colored pencils, crayons, or ballpoint pens. Markers will bleed through to the other side.
• Write, color, and draw in this book! Take notes. Expressing your thoughts in writing is a powerful way to create your reality. Here are some ideas of what to write: *Your day-to-day-mundane appointments. Daily gratitude. Daily reflections. Daily tarot. A diary of your spiritual journey. Intuitive messages. How you feel during different moon phases.*
• "Spellcasting Basics" are included to show you how to cast a circle, ground and center, and perform a "full" spell. If you are new to spells, please be sure to read this.
• And remember, the magic is inside you. Even if you start this book "late" or if it's not "the best" moon phase for a spell, you are the real power behind your magical life.

GOALS, PLANS, AND INTENTIONS

Yes, this is a planner, but that doesn't mean you have to get intense about... planning. You can even plan to do less this year. In fact, that's a great idea. Get to know what *you* want (not your family, not society, etc....) and then use the powers of magic and intention to focus your energy on those things. Here are some tips:
• Less is more. Go for broader feelings and intentions rather than super specific dates, processes, and outcomes. Leave room for magic to surprise you in fantastic ways.
• Make your goals as big or small as you want.
• Instead of saying what you don't want, "to stop being an emotional wreck," phrase it positively so you feel good when you say it, "to feel at ease with all of my emotions."
• Any plans you make are more of a guideline. Don't be afraid to scrap them and do something else if they don't feel right anymore. It's never too late to change directions or make new plans—in fact, that's often where the real magic comes into play.

HOW TO DO Magic

THE COSMOS
... and all things outside of your "control" ...

... LIKE OTHER PEOPLE & OUTSIDE INFLUENCES.

How do you use magic in real life?! By "stirring the cauldron" in your sphere of influence. Intention is the strongest magical power that you have. Simply put, intention means focusing your desire and energies towards what you want.

Since you're a powerful witch, you're always creating your reality. *So is it all your fault?!* No. Absolutely not. You're not the only one putting out energy and intentions. Everyone is. And our planes of reality are constantly feeling the influence of "outside" energies. Lots of stuff happens that you had no intention of creating.

Does that mean you're helpless against these outside forces? *Nope!* Outside influences are strong. But guess what... your sphere of influence is mighty strong, too. And you can also find ways to work with outside influences (like Astrology).

It's your job (if you choose to accept it!) to stir the contents of your own cauldron of intention toward what you desire. The illustration on the

DIVINE

PSYCHIC

MENTAL

EMOTIONAL

Stir That Cauldron!

PHYSICAL REALM

Your sphere of influence

right-hand page showcases your powers.

The physical realm is your body, your home, your stuff, and your spellcasting ingredients like herbs and candles. The emotional realm is your frequency that vibrates with your feelings. The mental realm is the energy of your thoughts. The psychic realm is interconnectedness, where you send out all of these energies into the universe and where you receive intuitive guidance and knowledge. And the divine realm is the level of universal or divine consciousness, your true self, your soul, and connectedness with "all" that is.

So, what do you do with this? Keep stirring your "cauldron" and aligning your intention, energies, and actions towards your desired outcome.

You'll go deeper into all of these powers as this book progresses, but for now, start noticing your actions, emotions, thoughts, intuitive guidance, and the calling of your soul. Then keep stirring your cauldron toward what you desire.

SPELLCASTING

TO SEE
Candles illuminate situations and spells.

to Release & BANISH
Scissors, flames, and burying things in the earth release energy.

TO GROW
Your garden and your imagination can help energy grow in spells.

To Create
Enliven the energy of what you wish to create with fiery spells and rituals.

TO ATTRACT
Similar energy attracts! Use your own vibration as well as the energy of crystals "charged" with your intentions.

TO CLEAR & CLEANSE
Bathings, sweeping, and moving energy with air or smoke can amplify your intentions of clearing and cleansing.

& INTENTIONS

Not a complete list.
Add your own!

TO EMPOWER

Crystals, wands, and the power of
your own hands, body, and actions
can empower your spells.

to Listen

Use tarot cards, gaze at reflective surfaces,
and most importantly, feel and listen very
closely to your emotions and energetic body.

TO HEAL

Sewing, mending, and
accepting what's passed
will help to heal.

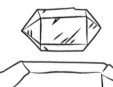

To Protect

Use herbs, circles, and symbols
of knots and "unbroken" lines
to protect your energy.

TO SEEK

Reading, listening, and asking
"to know" will provide the
answers you seek.

To Know

Intuitive wisdom is
already yours. Feel for
the knowing in your body.

To Wish

Gaze at the moon, the stars, and
most of all, believe that your dreams
and desires can come true.

Not a complete list. Add your own!

-Herbs-
Natural Magic

-Writings-
Intention

-Water-
Blessing & Purifying

-Sewing-
Creation &
Mending

-Metals-
Conducting Energy

Salt
Protection &
Purification

-Tea & Food-
Everyday Magic

-Books-
Knowledge

-Candles-
Illumination
& Energy

-Sacred Geometry-
Patterns of Life

& MAGIC SUPPLIES

TYPES OF SPELLS

GARDEN

Visualization

BLESSING

Altar
& SACRED
SPACE

DIRECTING
ENERGY

BATHING

Candles
& FIRE

Art

& RITUAL IDEAS

Not a complete list. Add your own!

Intention

INCENSE

Sewing

Herbs

EXPERIENCING NATURE & THE COSMOS

KITCHEN & TEA

Writing

THE ELEMENTS

SPIRIT
CONNECTION TO THE DIVINE SOURCE, DIVINE WITHIN, OR TRUE SELF.

WATER
EMOTION, INTUITION, AND CLEANSING RELEASE.

AIR
KNOWLEDGE, IDEAS, EXPANSION, AND COMMUNICATION.

EARTH
BELONGING, SECURITY, AND ABUNDANCE OF RESOURCES.

FIRE
CREATIVITY, LOVE, INSPIRATION, AND DESTROYING TO RE-CREATE.

- and the -

THE PENTACLE

THE ZODIAC

CAPRICORN (10)
"ACTIVE PRACTICALITY"
RULED BY SATURN.
STRUCTURED
& FOCUSED.
SUN:
DEC. 22–JAN. 19

SAGITTARIUS (9)
"ADAPTABLE ENTHUSIASM"
RULED BY JUPITER.
EXPLORATORY &
ENLIGHTENING.
SUN:
NOV. 22–DEC. 21

AQUARIUS (11)
"DETERMINED INTELLECTUAL"
RULED BY URANUS.
ECCENTRIC &
HUMANITARIAN.
SUN:
JAN. 20–FEB. 18

SCORPIO (8)
"DETERMINED FEELINGS"
RULED BY PLUTO.
TRANSFORMATIVE
& SPIRITUAL.
SUN:
OCT. 23–NOV. 21

PISCES (12)
"ADAPTABLE FEELINGS"
RULED BY NEPTUNE.
CREATIVE, DREAMY,
& SENSITIVE.
SUN:
FEB. 19–MAR. 20

LIBRA (7)
"ACTIVE INTELLECTUAL"
RULED BY VENUS.
BALANCED, SOCIAL,
& FAIR.
SUN:
SEPT. 23–OCT. 22

ARIES (1)
"ACTIVE INSPIRATION"
RULED BY MARS.
AMBITIOUS &
MOTIVATED.
SUN:
MAR. 21–APRIL 19

VIRGO (6)
"ADAPTABLE PRACTICALITY"
RULED BY MERCURY.
DETAILED &
ORGANIZED.
SUN:
AUG. 23–SEPT. 22

TAURUS (2)
"DETERMINED PRACTICALITY"
RULED BY VENUS.
COMFORTABLE &
GROUNDED.
SUN:
APRIL 20–MAY 20

LEO (5)
"PERSISTENT ENTHUSIASM"
RULED BY THE SUN.
CREATIVE, BOLD,
& PASSIONATE.
SUN:
JULY 23–AUG. 22

GEMINI (3)
"ADAPTABLE INTELLECT"
RULED BY MERCURY.
COMMUNICATIVE
& RESILIENT.
SUN:
MAY 21–JUNE 20

CANCER (4)
"ACTIVE FEELINGS"
RULED BY THE MOON.
INTROSPECTIVE
& INTUITIVE.
SUN:
JUNE 21–JULY 22

THE SECRETS OF

YOUR FEELINGS ARE THE SECRET SAUCE

To make real magic happen, combine actions (things that you do), intentions (also known as feelings or emotions), as well as powers outside of yourself, such as the moon and nature. This chart will give you some ideas on how to feel and set your intentions.

An intention is when you strongly feel what you desire in your body, as if you already have it.

You can use the phases of the moon to "pull the thread" of magic forward by listening to your feelings and continually refocusing these intentions with actions to match.

Since the moon and emotions are both linked to the subconscious, *you'll use your body to feel these things and set intentions*, not your thoughts in your conscious mind.

FIRST QUARTER

Feel where you would like to change, grow, or expand. Allow yourself to dream and imagine what it might be like to make a change, even if it doesn't seem possible right now.

WAXING CRESCENT

Feel what excites you and sparks a sense of curiosity. Ask questions and look for answers, clues, patterns, and coincidences. Use the subtle feelings of what "lights you up" to set intentions and guide your actions.

NEW MOON

Allow yourself to feel where you are judging yourself. When you are ready, forgive yourself and let the energy shift until you find a place of neutrality and self-acceptance.

MOON MAGIC

FULL MOON

Reaffirm your visions and intentions until the energy of what you desire begins to feel real.

If you feel clarity, make decisions to move forward quickly. If you feel confusion, illuminate your emotions through writing, ritual, divination, movement, etc.

Ask: What am I missing? What am I feeling?

LAST QUARTER

Allow yourself to feel what's working, and what isn't. Let your feelings flow to a place of ease and trust in yourself, so you can discern what you want and what you do not want.

WANING CRESCENT

Feel the relief as you realize that some thoughts and feelings are unnecessary. Intend to let those things go, and then see what you have left. Let your intentions flow to a place of release.

DARK

Let the darkness filter out noise and distractions. Take a step back from actions and thoughts. Allow the dark moon to reset your mind, body, and spirit with the energy of rest.

the correspondence of
THE MOON AND SEASONS

The moon completes a full cycle of its phases in just over 28 days, which is relatively quick. One moon cycle is perfect for shorter projects and immediate goals.

You can also "correspond" these shorter moon phases to a longer-term cycle, the seasons, also known as the Wheel of the Year. This longer cycle is useful for "big" goals and plans that'll take more than a month.

While the seasons and sun embody more of a conscious or outward energy, the moon is subconscious or internal. However, they both follow a similar cycle and progression of dark to light.

The handy chart on the following page demonstrates that the phases of the moon correspond to an energy point on the Wheel of the Year. This pattern of energy—the waxing and waning of light—is no coincidence. It's the pattern and flow of the creative force of the universe. This process and cycle is how magic "works."

Here's an overview of the eight sabbats and a chart that connects them to the moon phases and seasons.

IMBOLC: February 1 or 2. Imbolc is the time to celebrate the first signs of spring or the return of the sun's increasing light. This sabbat corresponds to the waxing crescent moon.

OSTARA: March 20. This sabbat is celebrated on the spring equinox. Witches often mark this day with a ritual planting of seeds. Ostara corresponds to the first quarter moon.

BELTANE: May 1. Beltane is a time for rituals of growth, creation, and taking action to make things happen. This sabbat corresponds to the waxing gibbous moon.

LITHA: June 20. This sabbat celebrates the summer solstice, when the sun is at its strongest. Litha is a time of great magical and personal power and corresponds to the full moon.

LUGHNASADH: August 1. This day is a celebration of the "first harvest" where we gather early grains, herbs, fruits, and vegetables from the earth. It corresponds to the waning gibbous moon, where light and power begin to descend from their fullest stage.

MABON: September 21. Celebrated on the autumnal equinox, this sabbat is about release, balance, and letting go. It is the second harvest and corresponds to the last quarter moon.

SAMHAIN: October 31. Samhain is a celebration of the dark half of the year. It is a time to cast spells of protection for the upcoming winter. It corresponds to the waning crescent moon.

YULE: December 21. Marked by the winter solstice and the shortest (darkest) day of the year, this sabbat corresponds to the dark and new moon.

A NOTE ABOUT THE CROSS-QUARTER DATES AND SOUTHERN HEMISPHERE SEASONS:

CROSS QUARTER DATES: The dates for the two solstices and two equinoxes each year—Ostara, Litha, Mabon, and Yule—are calculated astronomically, from the position of the earth to the sun. The "cross quarter" festivals, which are the points between—Imbolc, Beltane, Lughnasadh, and Samhain—are often celebrated on "fixed" dates instead of the actual midpoints. This book lists both the "Fixed Festival Dates," where it's more common to celebrate, and the "Astronomical Dates." Choose either date or any time in between for your own ritual. 'Tis the season for magic.

SOUTHERN HEMISPHERE SEASONS: If you're on the "southern" half of the Earth, like in Australia, the seasonal shifts are opposite on the calendar year. So you'll feel the energy of the summer solstice (corresponding to the full moon) in December instead of June, and so on.

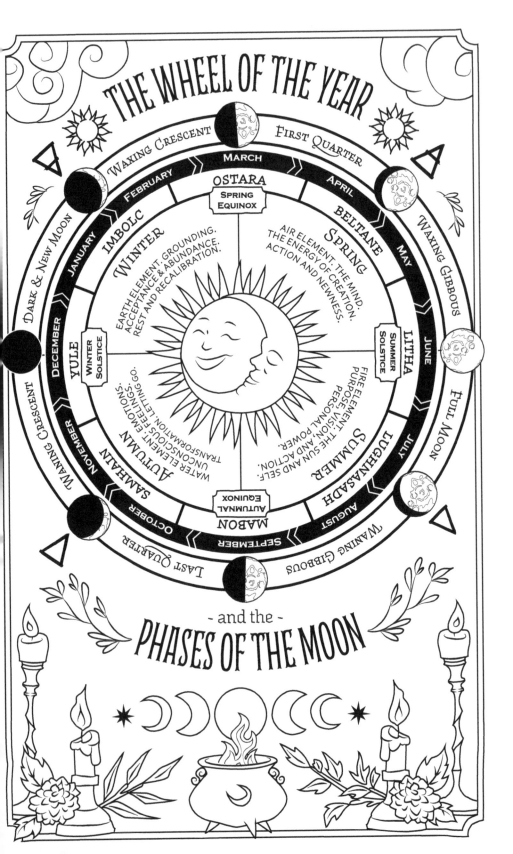

Spellcasting Basics

There are opening and closing steps that are basic accompaniments to spells in this book. These steps are optional but advisable: at least know "why" many witches perform these processes and try them out for yourself.

And keep in mind, this is a super basic "coloring book" guide to the spellcasting process. There are books and online sources that go much further in-depth.

THE SECRET OF SPELLS

The secret to powerful spells is in you. Your feeling and vibration in alignment with your true source of self—and/or a higher power—is what makes spells work.

The secret isn't in having the right ingredients and doing all the steps in a particular order. It's in your ability to focus your intent and use your feelings, mind, and soul to call in what you want—to harness the energy of yourself in harmony with the Earth, stars, moon, planets, or whatever other spiritual forces you call upon.

BREAK THE RULES

The first rule is to throw out any of the rules that don't work for you. Do things that feel right, significant, and meaningful. Adapt spells from different practices, books, and teachers. The only

way to know what works is to follow your curiosity and try things out.

USING TOOLS

Your feelings and vibration are what unlocks the magic, not the tools, exact words, or sequences. You can cast amazing spells for free with no tools at all, and you can cast an elaborate spell that yields no results.

That said, tools like herbs, oils, crystals, and cauldrons can be powerful and fun to use in your spells. Just don't feel pressured or discouraged if you don't have much to start. Keep your magic straightforward and powerful. The right tools and ingredients will come.

"AS ABOVE, SO BELOW"

Tools, ingredients, and symbols are based on the magical theory of sympathetic magic and correspondence. You might hear the phrase, "As Above, So Below," which means the spiritual qualities of objects are passed down to earth. It's "sympathetic magic," or "this equals that," like how a figure of a lion represents that power but is not an actual lion.

Start by following lists, charts, and spells to get a feel for what others use and then begin to discover your own meaningful symbolism and correspondences.

PERMISSION

Spellbooks are like guidelines. They should be modified, simplified, or embellished to your liking. And don't degrade your magic by calling it "lazy." Keeping your witchcraft simple is okay. Go ahead, you have permission.

Also, it's not a competition to see who can use the most esoteric stuff in their spell. Hooray! It's about finding your personal power and style.

SPELLCASTING OUTLINE:

1. Plan and prepare.
2. Cast a circle.
3. Ground and center.
4. Invoke a deity or connection to self.
5. Raise energy.
6. Do your spellcraft (like the spells in this book).
7. Ground and center again.
8. Close your circle.
9. Clean up.
10. Act in accord (and be patient).

1. PLAN AND PREPARE: If you're doing a written spell, read it several times to get familiar with it. Decide if there's anything you'll substitute or change. If you're writing your own spell, enjoy the process and mystery of seeing the messages and theme come together.

Gather all of the items you'll be using (if any) and plan out the space and time where you'll do the spell. Spells can be impromptu, so preparations can be quick and casual if you like.

2. CAST A CIRCLE AND CALL THE QUARTERS: A magic circle is a container to collect the energy of your spell. Circles are also protective, as they form a ring or "barrier" around you. Circles can elevate your space to a higher vibration and clear out unwanted energy before you begin. Calling the Quarters is done to get the universal energies of the elements flowing. Incense is typically burned at the same time to purify the air and energy. If you

can't burn things, that's ok. If you've never cast a circle, try it. It's a mystical experience like no other. Once you have a few candles lit and start to walk around it, magic does happen!

HOW TO CAST A CIRCLE: This is a basic, bare-bones way to cast a circle. It's often much more elaborate, and this explanation barely does it justice, so read up to find out more. And note that while some cast the circle first and then call the Quarters, some do it the other way around.

1. Hold out your hand, wand, or crystal, and imagine a white light and a sphere of pure energy surrounding your space, as you circle around clockwise three times. Your circle can be large or it can be tiny, just space for you and your materials.

2. Call the Four Quarters or Five Points of the Pentagram, depending on your preferences. The Quarters (also known as the Elements!) are Earth (North), Air (East), Fire (South), and Water (West). Many use the Pentagram and also call the 5th Element, Spirit or Self.

Face in each direction and say a few words to welcome the element. For example, "To the North, I call upon the power of grounding and strength. To the East, I call upon the source of knowledge. To the South, I call upon the passion and burning desire to take action. To the West, I call upon the intuition of emotion. To the Spirit and Source of Self, I call upon the guidance and light."

3. GROUND AND CENTER: Grounding and centering prepare you to use the energy from the Earth, elements, and universe. Most witches agree that if you skip these steps, you'll be drawing off of your own energy, which can be exhausting and ineffective. It's wise to ground and center both before and after a spell. It's like the difference between being "plugged into" the magical energy of the Earth and universe versus "draining your batteries."

HOW TO GROUND AND CENTER:

To ground, imagine the energy coming up from the core of the Earth and into your feet, as you breathe deeply. You can visualize deep roots from your feet all the way into the center of the Earth, with these roots drawing the Earth's energy in and out of you. The point is to allow these great channels of energy to flow through you and into your spell. You can also imagine any of your negative energy, thoughts, or stress leaving.

To center, once you've got a good flow of energy from the ground, imagine the energy shining through and out the top of your head as a pure form of your highest creative self and then back in as the light of guidance. Suspend yourself here between the Earth and the sky, supported with the energy flowing freely through you, upheld, balanced, cleansed, and "in flow" with the energy of the universe. This process takes just a couple of minutes.

4. INVOKE A DEITY OR CREATIVE SOURCE: If you'd like to invoke a deity or your highest self to help raise energy and your vibration, call upon them. Invoking deities is way deeper than this book, so research it more if it calls to you!

5. RAISE ENERGY: The point of raising energy is to channel the universal (magical!) forces you tapped into through the previous steps to use in your spell. And raising energy is fun. You can sing, dance, chant, meditate, or do breath work. You want to do something that feels natural, so you can really get into it, lose yourself, and raise your state of consciousness.

A good way to start is to chant "Ong," allowing the roof of your mouth to vibrate ever so slightly. This vibration changes up the energy in your mind, body, and breath and is a simple yet powerful technique.

Another tip is to raise energy to the point of the "peak" where you feel it at its highest. Don't go too far where you start to tucker out or lose enthusiasm!

6. DO YOUR SPELL: Your spell can be as simple as saying an intention and focusing on achieving the outcome of what you want, or it can be more elaborate. Whichever way you prefer, do what feels right to you.

TIPS ON VISUALIZATION AND INTENTION:

Most spellwork involves a bit of imagination and intention, and here are some subtleties you can explore.

The Power of You The most important tool in magic is you. You've got it—both power right now and vast untapped power that you can explore. To cast a successful spell, you've got to focus your mind and genuinely feel the emotions and feelings of the things you want to manifest.

If you haven't started meditating in some form yet, start now! It's not too late, and it's easier than you think.

Visualize the Outcome

Visualization doesn't have to be visual. In fact, *feeling* the outcome of what you want may be more effective than seeing it (try both). And try to feel or see the *completion* of your desire without worrying about the process or *how* you'll get there.

If you don't know how you're going to achieve your goal (yet!), it can feel overwhelming when you try to visualize how you're going to pull it off. Instead, feel the sense of calm, completion, and control that you'll feel *after* you achieve it.

Phrase it Positively

Another tip is to phrase your intentions and desires positively. You're putting energy into this, so make sure the intention is going to be good for you. Instead of saying what you don't want, "to get out of my bad job that I hate," phrase it positively, "I want to do something that's fulfilling with my career."

Then you'll be able to feel good about it as you visualize and cast your spell.

7. GROUND AND CENTER AGAIN

After your spell, it's important to ground out any excess energy. Do this again by visualizing energy flowing through you and out. You can also imagine any "extra" energy you have petering out as you release it back into the Earth.

8. CLOSE YOUR CIRCLE

If you called the Quarters or a deity, let them know the spell has ended by calling them out again, with thanks if desired.

Close your circle the opposite of how you opened it, circling around three times or more counterclockwise. Then say, "This circle is closed," or do a closing chant or song to finish your spell.

9. CLEAN UP

Don't be messy with your magic! Put away all of your spell items.

10. ACT IN ACCORD: Once you have cast your spell, you've got to take action. You can cast a spell to become a marine biologist, but if you don't study for it, it's never going to happen. So take action towards what you want to open the possibility for it to come.

Look for signs, intuition, and coincidences that point you in the direction of your desires. If you get inspired after a spell, take action! Don't be surprised if you ask for money and then come up with a new idea to make money. Follow those clues, especially if they feel exciting and good.

If your spell comes true, discard and "release" any charm bag, poppet, or item you used to hold and amplify energy. Also, give thanks (if that's in your practice) or repay the universe in some way, doing something kind or of service that you feel is a solid trade for what you received from your spell.

WHAT IF YOUR SPELL DOESN'T WORK?

It's true that not all spells will work! But sometimes the results just take longer than you'd like, so be patient.

If your spell doesn't work, you can use divination or meditation to do some digging into reasons why.

The good news is your own magic, power, frequency, and intention is still on your side. You can try again and add more energy in the direction of your desired outcome by casting another spell.

Give it some deep thought. What else is at play? Did you really take inspired action? Are you totally honest with yourself about what you want? Are there any thoughts or feelings about your spell that feel "off"? Are you grateful for what you already have? Can you "give back" or reciprocate with service or energy?

FOR MORE TIPS AND INSPIRATION:

Seek out websites, books, podcasts, and videos on spirituality. Follow your intuition and curiosity to deepen your practice and find your own style. And check out other books in the *Coloring Book of Shadows* series, like the *Book of Spells* and *Witch Life*.

SOUTHERN HEMISPHERE MAGIC

If you're in the Southern Hemisphere in a place like Australia, there are a couple of differences that you'll need to note.

The biggest difference is that since seasonal shifts are opposite on the calendar year, you'll feel the energy of Samhain around May 1 instead of October 31.

Southern Hemisphere "spinning and circle casting" will go "sun wise" according to the south—counterclockwise for invoking (drawing in), clockwise for banishing (letting go).

North and South Elements are also typically swapped in Southern Hemisphere magic—North = Fire, South = Earth.

SO MOTE IT BE.

Your Magical Vision

AND PLANS FOR THIS YEAR:

Remember that plans almost always change. So try to envision what you can influence no matter what, and don't worry about deadlines. Magic works in its own time.

- Who do you want to be this year?
- What do you want this year to feel like?
- What do you want to take action on or work towards?
- What steps, thoughts, actions, and feelings will get you going in the direction that you desire?
- What does success feel and look like to you?
- What do you really want that you are hesitant to ask for?

Reach for the Stars

THINGS YOU CAN CONTROL: *Nothing!* You can't control anything, but you can influence, plan, and make things better for yourself and for the world. You matter, and your magic and energy matter.

THINGS YOU CAN INFLUENCE OR CHANGE: Your priorities, your actions, your thoughts, how you spend some of your time, the collective consciousness, and the spiritual evolution of the planet. Ultimately, you can influence how you feel after you've processed and felt all of your feelings just as they are.

As Above...

1ST HALF 2024

January

S	M	T	W	Th	F	Sa
	1	2	◑	4	5	6
7	8	9	10	●	12	13
14	15	16	◐	18	19	20
21	22	23	24	○	26	27
28	29	30	31			

February

S	M	T	W	Th	F	Sa
				1	◑	3
4	5	6	7	8	●	10
11	12	13	14	15	◐	17
18	19	20	21	22	23	○
25	26	27	28	29		

March

S	M	T	W	Th	F	Sa
					1	2
◑	4	5	6	7	8	9
●	11	12	13	14	15	16
◐	18	19	20	21	22	23
24	○	26	27	28	29	30
31						

April

S	M	T	W	Th	F	Sa
	◑	2	3	4	5	6
7	●	9	10	11	12	13
14	◐	16	17	18	19	20
21	22	○	24	25	26	27
28	29	30				

May

S	M	T	W	Th	F	Sa
			◑	2	3	4
5	6	●	8	9	10	11
12	13	14	◐	16	17	18
19	20	21	22	○	24	25
26	27	28	29	◐	31	

June

S	M	T	W	Th	F	Sa
						1
2	3	4	5	●	7	8
9	10	11	12	13	◐	15
16	17	18	19	20	○	22
23	24	25	26	27	◐	29
30						

2ND HALF 2024

July

S	M	T	W	Th	F	Sa
	1	2	3	4	●	6
7	8	9	10	11	12	◐
14	15	16	17	18	19	20
○	22	23	24	25	26	◑
28	29	30	31			

August

S	M	T	W	Th	F	Sa
				1	2	3
●	5	6	7	8	9	10
11	◐	13	14	15	16	17
18	○	20	21	22	23	24
25	◑	27	28	29	30	31

September

S	M	T	W	Th	F	Sa
1	●	3	4	5	6	7
8	9	10	◐	12	13	14
15	16	○	18	19	20	21
22	23	◑	25	26	27	28
29	30					

October

S	M	T	W	Th	F	Sa
		1	●	3	4	5
6	7	8	9	◐	11	12
13	14	15	16	○	18	19
20	21	22	23	◑	25	26
27	28	29	30	31		

November

S	M	T	W	Th	F	Sa
					●	2
3	4	5	6	7	8	◐
10	11	12	13	14	○	16
17	18	19	20	21	◑	23
24	25	26	27	28	29	30

December

S	M	T	W	Th	F	Sa
●	2	3	4	5	6	7
◐	9	10	11	12	13	14
○	16	17	18	19	20	21
◑	23	24	25	26	27	28
29	●	31				

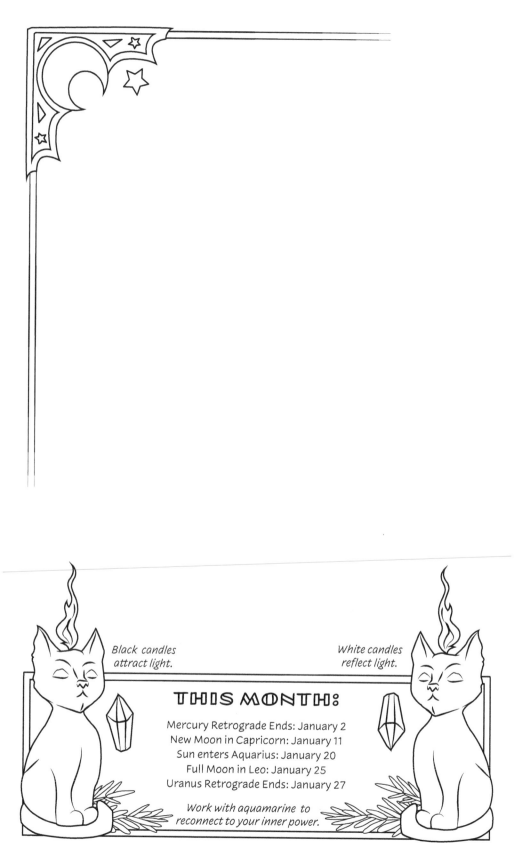

Black candles
attract light.

White candles
reflect light.

THIS MONTH:

Mercury Retrograde Ends: January 2
New Moon in Capricorn: January 11
Sun enters Aquarius: January 20
Full Moon in Leo: January 25
Uranus Retrograde Ends: January 27

*Work with aquamarine to
reconnect to your inner power.*

-Willow Broom-
Witch Power

-Star of the Muses-
Sacred Power
& Inspiration

Drink spicy teas
to enliven your
senses.

Burn
sandalwood
to empower
your spirit.

Wear a conical hat to
channel your power.

JANUARY

CLAIMING YOUR POWER

Feel a glimmer of your witch power by deciding
that it's possible for your dreams to come true.

Hold your breath. Make a wish. Count to three.

What does your heart desire?

Claiming Your Power
A Spell to Activate Your Magic

The first four spells in the book delve into your inner power. This power is all you need to make magic happen, and it's already within you.

PREPARE an optional sacred space. The only requirement is your own self and body, existing right now as you are. If you want to embellish: light candles, burn incense like bay, sage, clove, or lemon verbena, or drink ginger or peppermint tea. You can also hold a crystal like quartz, citrine, or amethyst to help you feel your magic.

CAST YOUR SPELL. With your hand over your heart, claim what you desire or who you wish to be. Make your wish*. Decide that you can have it, and that it is possible, even if there are many steps (or obstacles) before you get there.

When you make your wish, you'll feel a spark of energy, a glimmer inside of you. That is the spark of magic. Feel that internally, even if for a split-second, and you will spark the cauldron of magic that is within you and available to you anytime, anywhere, and in any circumstance.

Once you feel that spark, aim to sit with it for a moment. Feel it flowing to you and through you, from the ground up through your body and out of the top of your head.

Repeat this spell anytime you feel lost or disconnected from your magic and intentions.

The next steps to make magic happen are to flow and "dance" with this energy as it manifests... which you'll do in the following spells.

*Aww, sorry! You can't wish people back from the dead or make someone specific fall in love with you. Your wish must comply with the laws of physics, biology, and free will for it to come true.

JANUARY 2024

	SUNDAY	MONDAY	TUESDAY
	31	1	2
	7	8	9
	14	15	16
	21	22	23
	28	29	30

-Charoite-

INTENTIONS
Claim Your Desire for Magic.

-Vervain-

WEDNESDAY	THURSDAY	FRIDAY	SATURDAY
3 Last Quarter ◐	4	5	6
10	11 New Moon ●♑	12	13
			☉ Sun in Aquarius ≈≈
17 First Quarter ◑	18	19	20
24	25 Full Moon ○ ♌	26	27
	★ Imbolc (Fixed Date)		
31	1	2 Last Quarter ◐	3

JANUARY 2024

MONDAY, JANUARY 1

TUESDAY, JANUARY 2
► Moon void-of-course begins 6:36 PM EST
Moon enters Libra ♎ 7:47 PM EST
☿℞ Mercury Retrograde ends

WEDNESDAY, JANUARY 3
Last Quarter ☽ 10:30 PM EST

THURSDAY, JANUARY 4

FRIDAY, JANUARY 5
► Moon void-of-course begins 6:41 AM EST
Moon enters Scorpio ♏ 7:39 AM EST

SATURDAY, JANUARY 6

SUNDAY, JANUARY 7
► Moon void-of-course begins 3:22 PM EST
Moon enters Sagittarius ♐ 4:08 PM EST

Hold citrine to your heart or solar plexus
to know your desires and inner wisdom.

JANUARY 2024

MONDAY, JANUARY 8

TUESDAY, JANUARY 9
►Moon void-of-course begins 1:25 PM EST
Moon enters Capricorn ♑ 8:33 PM EST

WEDNESDAY, JANUARY 10

THURSDAY, JANUARY 11
New Moon ● ♑ 6:57 AM EST
►Moon void-of-course begins 9:33 PM EST
Moon enters Aquarius ♒ 10:01 PM EST

FRIDAY, JANUARY 12

SATURDAY, JANUARY 13
►Moon void-of-course begins 4:59 AM EST
Moon enters Pisces ♓ 10:29 PM EST

SUNDAY, JANUARY 14

INNER POWER

Use an elder wand or broom to feel a sense of empowerment

JANUARY 2024

MONDAY, JANUARY 15
▶Moon void-of-course begins 11:33 PM EST
Moon enters Aries ♈ 11:49 PM EST

TUESDAY, JANUARY 16

WEDNESDAY, JANUARY 17
First Quarter ☽ 10:53 PM EST

THURSDAY, JANUARY 18
▶Moon void-of-course begins 3:03 AM EST
Moon enters Taurus ♉ 3:12 AM EST

FRIDAY, JANUARY 19

SATURDAY, JANUARY 20
▶Moon void-of-course begins 8:57 AM EST
Moon enters Gemini ♊ 8:58 AM EST
☉ Sun enters Aquarius ♒ 9:07 AM EST

SUNDAY, JANUARY 21

*Light a black or purple candle
and intend to learn something
new and valuable about magic.*

JANUARY 2024

MONDAY, JANUARY 22
►Moon void-of-course begins 3:40 PM EST
Moon enters Cancer ♋ 4:51 PM EST

TUESDAY, JANUARY 23

WEDNESDAY, JANUARY 24
►Moon void-of-course begins 5:58 PM EST

THURSDAY, JANUARY 25
Moon enters Leo ♌ 2:37 AM EST
Full Moon ○ ♌ 12:57 PM EST

FRIDAY, JANUARY 26
►Moon void-of-course begins 4:19 PM EST

SATURDAY, JANUARY 27
Moon enters Virgo ♍ 2:11 PM EST
♅℞ Uranus Retrograde ends

SUNDAY, JANUARY 28

CAT

*Channel cat energy
to focus your
witch power.*

JANUARY 2024/FEBRUARY 2024

MONDAY, JANUARY 29
►Moon void-of-course begins 6:20 PM EST

TUESDAY, JANUARY 30
Moon enters Libra ♎ 3:04 AM EST

WEDNESDAY, JANUARY 31

THURSDAY, FEBRUARY 1
★ Imbolc (Fixed Festival Date)
►Moon void-of-course begins 4:03 AM EST
Moon enters Scorpio ♏ 3:37 PM EST

FRIDAY, FEBRUARY 2
Last Quarter ◑ 6:18 PM EST

SATURDAY, FEBRUARY 3
►Moon void-of-course begins 10:24 PM EST

SUNDAY, FEBRUARY 4
Moon enters Sagittarius ♐ 1:28 AM EST
★ Imbolc (Astronomical Date) 3:28 AM EST

IMBOLC

Feel the magic of a fresh start. Try bathing or cleaning with enlivening herbs (basil or mint) and purifying herbs (agrimony and witch hazel.)

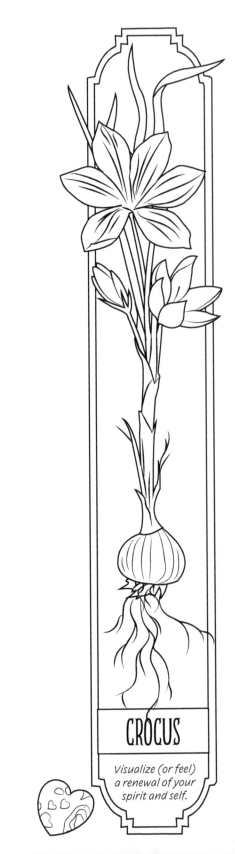

CROCUS

*Visualize (or feel)
a renewal of your
spirit and self.*

Light a candle and watch the darkness define the light.

- Ravens -
Wisdom of the Dark

THIS MONTH:

Imbolc: February 1-4
New Moon in Aquarius: February 9
Sun enters Pisces: February 18
Full Moon in Virgo: February 24

Onyx can heal & reveal trauma from the past.

- Magic Hexagram -
The polarity of light
and dark.

Burn rosemary
to recall who
you are.

Make a list of
dreams yet to be
fulfilled.

Carry a silver key to
unlock lost joy.

- Labradorite -
Self-Discovery

Protect your space with birch
incense or a birch broom.

Place thistles on your altar to
guide your shadow work.

FEBRUARY
POWER OF SHADOW
Rediscover the magic of your shadows
through intuition and self-acceptance.
Allow your secret desires to come to light.

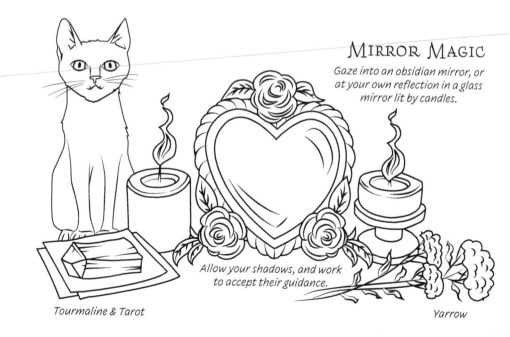

Mirror Magic

Gaze into an obsidian mirror, or at your own reflection in a glass mirror lit by candles.

Allow your shadows, and work to accept their guidance.

Tourmaline & Tarot

Yarrow

Love Your Shadow

Facing Your Shadow
Finding Power in the Darkness

When you think about who you are and what you desire, there might be a bit of "yeah, but...!" in the back of your mind. This tiny voice of doubt is shadowy gold—it points directly to a vital part of yourself that you are hesitant to face.

In shadow work, you might uncover false beliefs about why you can't have what you truly desire, or maybe you'll see possibilities you've hidden because of shame or fear.

For example, "art" as a shadow could mean you're afraid you're not good enough to be an artist. You might have given up on art and may be jealous of others. The point is to uncover and accept these desires without judgment or shame.

CAST THE SPELL: At midnight, light a black candle behind you and gaze into a mirror so you see the candle. Or just sit in near-total darkness.

Then answer the following questions (record and play them back on your phone if it's dark!).

1. What do you desire that you think you cannot have?

2. Why do you think you cannot have it?

3. If it was possible for you, how could it be possible?

4. What do you have to accept for it to come true?

5. What do you have to forgive in yourself to accept that this desire is possible for you?

Extra Credit of Darkness: Who or what are you jealous of?

Once you've uncovered a shadow, ask: what were you trying to protect yourself from by hiding this shadow, and why? Explain the reasons to your shadow self, and be honest.

Then come up with first steps on how you can gently reincorporate this shadow back into your life, if and when you are ready.

FEBRUARY 2024

	SUNDAY	MONDAY	TUESDAY
	28	29	30
	★ Imbolc 3:28 AM EST 4	5	6
	11	12	13
	☉ Sun enters Pisces ♓ 18	19	20
	25	26	27

WEDNESDAY	THURSDAY	FRIDAY	SATURDAY
	★ Imbolc (Fixed Date)		
31	1	2 Last Quarter ◑	3
7	8	9 New Moon ● ≈	10
14	15	16 First Quarter ◑	17
21	22	23	24 Full Moon ○ ♍
28	29	1	2

FEBRUARY 2024

MONDAY, FEBRUARY 5

TUESDAY, FEBRUARY 6
► Moon void of course begins 12:06 AM EST
Moon enters Capricorn ♑ 7:09 AM EST

WEDNESDAY, FEBRUARY 7

THURSDAY, FEBRUARY 8
► Moon void of course begins 2:52 AM EST
Moon enters Aquarius ♒ 8:59 AM EST

FRIDAY, FEBRUARY 9
► Moon void of course begins 5:59 PM EST
New Moon ● ♒ 5:59 PM EST

*Befriend your darkness
with licorice, chamomile,
and ginseng tea.*

SATURDAY, FEBRUARY 10
Moon enters Pisces ♓ 8:42 AM EST

SUNDAY, FEBRUARY 11

*Drink tea for self-love with dark
chocolate, mint, and marshmallow root.*

FEBRUARY 2024

MONDAY, FEBRUARY 12
▶ Moon void of course begins 7:31 AM EST
Moon enters Aries ♈ 8:26 AM EST

TUESDAY, FEBRUARY 13

WEDNESDAY, FEBRUARY 14
▶ Moon void of course begins 5:21 AM EST
Moon enters Taurus ♉ 10:02 AM EST

THURSDAY, FEBRUARY 15

FRIDAY, FEBRUARY 16
First Quarter ◐ 10:01 AM EST
▶ Moon void of course begins 10:01 AM EST
Moon enters Gemini ♊ 2:39 PM EST

SATURDAY, FEBRUARY 17

SUNDAY, FEBRUARY 18
▶ Moon void of course begins 10:21 PM EST
Moon enters Cancer ♋ 10:25 PM EST
☉ Sun enters Pisces ♓ 11:12 PM EST

DOG

*Channel dog energy
to accept yourself
just as you are.*

Smoky Quartz

FEBRUARY 2024

MONDAY, FEBRUARY 19

TUESDAY, FEBRUARY 20

WEDNESDAY, FEBRUARY 21
➤ Moon void of course begins 1:38 AM EST
Moon enters Leo ♌ 8:40 AM EST

THURSDAY, FEBRUARY 22
➤ Moon void of course begins 11:18 PM EST

FRIDAY, FEBRUARY 23
Moon enters Virgo ♍ 8:38 PM EST

Mugwort

SATURDAY, FEBRUARY 24
Full Moon ○ ♍ 7:30 AM EST

SUNDAY, FEBRUARY 25

- Black Witch Moth -
Messages from the Other Side

FEBRUARY/MARCH 2024

MONDAY, FEBRUARY 26
► Moon void of course begins 2:25 AM EST
Moon enters Libra ♎ 9:29 AM EST

TUESDAY, FEBRUARY 27
► Moon void of course begins 1:22 PM EST

WEDNESDAY, FEBRUARY 28
Moon enters Scorpio ♏ 10:09 P EST

THURSDAY, FEBRUARY 29

FRIDAY, MARCH 1

SATURDAY, MARCH 2
► Moon void of course begins 2:47AM EST
Moon enters Sagittarius ♐ 8:56 AM EST

SUNDAY, MARCH 3
Last Quarter ◑ 10:23 AM EST

NETTLE

*An all-purpose herb
for shadow work &
counter-magic.*

Drink green tea and ginseng for extra energy to take action.

THIS MONTH:

New Moon in Pisces: March 10
Ostara (Spring Equinox): March 19
Sun enters Aries: March 19
Full Moon in Libra: March 25
Lunar Eclipse: March 25

Calendar dates around arch: 29 1 2 3 4 5 6 7 8 9 10 11 12 13 14 15 16 17 18 19 20 21 22 23 24 25 26 27 28 29 30 31

Zodiac signs: SCORPIO SAGITT. CAPRI. AQUARI. PISCES ARIES TAURUS GEMINI CANCER LEO VIRGO LIBRA SCORPIO SAGITT.

PISCES

ARIES

- Triskellion -
The cycles of life,
death, and rebirth.

- Snake -
Transformation

Rub thyme oil on
your shoes for
courage.

Use an oak wand or broom
to cast strong intentions.

Burn bay leaves and candles
to empower your actions.

- Quartz -
Moving energy

MARCH

POWER OF INTENTION

Perform "The Crystal Dance" by dancing around
with crystals as you cast energetic intentions.
Amplify your intentions with movement and action.

Channel hawk energy
to focus and direct
your attention.

CASTING YOUR INTENTIONS
THE DANCE OF MAKING MAGIC

The new moon and spring equinox are auspicious times for intention-setting rituals, but intentions aren't a one-time, instant thing. Once you've set an intention, you've got to "dance" or move with that energy and take some steps and actions to manifest it.

PREPARE: Gather the clues you've collected from the two previous spells. Think deeply about what you desire outwardly and in the shadows. What is your intention? Write it down.

PERFORM THE RITUAL: Set up a ritual space in way that feels natural to you. For example, hold a crystal or light a white candle with a silver chain around it to amplify your intentions.

In your third eye, deeply feel your intention. Envision it if you can, but more importantly, immerse yourself in the feeling or energy of already having it. This is the feeling that you want to "lock in" so you can recall it later.

Spend a few minutes to deepen the sensation, then bring the feeling to the lower back of your head. If your neck gets tingly—awesome.

TAKE ONE ACTION: Your magical guidance (intuition) will always show you at least one step to take in the direction that you want to go. This next step is already in your physical realm and you already know what it is... so take that step. This is a nice reminder that you aren't pushing, you are flowing into what is already there.

HOLD THE ENERGY: It's okay to fall out of sync with the energy of your intentions, but do yourself a favor... reset those intentions by frequently recalling the feelings you generated in this ritual, and remember... You are a witch!

MARCH 2024

	SUNDAY	MONDAY	TUESDAY
	25	26	27
	3 Last Quarter ◑	4	5
	10 New Moon ● ♓	11	12
	17 First Quarter ◐	18	19 ★Ostara (Spring Equinox) ☉ Sun enters Aries ♈
	24	25 Full Moon ○ ♎ ★Penumbral Lunar Eclipse	26
	31	1 Last Quarter ◑	2

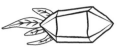

INTENTIONS
Visualize a Bright Future.

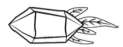

WEDNESDAY	THURSDAY	FRIDAY	SATURDAY
28	29	1	2
6	7	8	9
13	14	15	16
20	21	22	23
27	28	29	30
3	4	5	6

MARCH 2024

MONDAY, MARCH 4
▸ Moon void of course begins 10:41 AM EST
Moon enters Capricorn ♑ 4:15 PM EST

TUESDAY, MARCH 5

WEDNESDAY, MARCH 6
▸ Moon void of course begins 12:36 PM EST
Moon enters Aquarius ♒ 7:38 PM EST

THURSDAY, MARCH 7

FRIDAY, MARCH 8
▸ Moon void of course begins 1:56 PM EST
Moon enters Pisces ♓ 8:03 PM EST

SATURDAY, MARCH 9

SUNDAY, MARCH 10
New Moon ● ♓ 5:00 AM EDT
▸ Moon void of course begins 3:45 PM EDT
Moon enters Aries ♈ 8:19 PM EDT

Burn incense with bergamot, goldenrod, rose, and thyme for an uplifting boost.

MARCH 2024

MONDAY, MARCH 11

TUESDAY, MARCH 12
► Moon void of course begins 7:08 AM EDT
Moon enters Taurus ♉ 8:28 PM EDT

WEDNESDAY, MARCH 13

THURSDAY, MARCH 14
► Moon void of course begins 6:29 PM EDT
Moon enters Gemini ♊ 11:16 PM EDT

FRIDAY, MARCH 15

SATURDAY, MARCH 16

SUNDAY, MARCH 17
First Quarter ◑ 12:11 AM EST
► Moon void of course begins 12:43 AM EDT
Moon enters Cancer ♋ 5:40 AM EDT

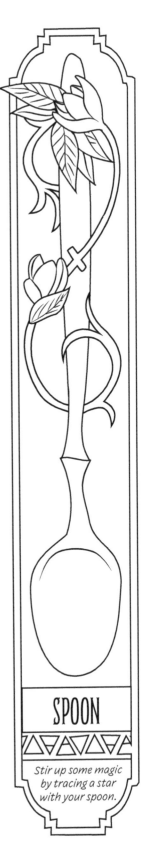

SPOON

*Stir up some magic
by tracing a star
with your spoon.*

MARCH 2024

MONDAY, MARCH 18

TUESDAY, MARCH 19
➤ Moon void of course begins 2:52 PM EDT
Moon enters Leo ♌ 3:33 PM EDT
★ Ostara (Spring Equinox) 11:07 PM EDT
☉ Sun enters Aries ♈ 11:06 PM EDT

WEDNESDAY, MARCH 20

THURSDAY, MARCH 21

FRIDAY, MARCH 22
➤ Moon void of course begins 2:34 AM EDT
Moon enters Virgo ♍ 3:42 AM EDT

SATURDAY, MARCH 23

SUNDAY, MARCH 24
➤ Moon void of course begins 11:49 AM EDT
Moon enters Libra ♎ 4:37 PM EDT

OSTARA
Feel the energy of exciting new possibilities.
Drink tea, burn incense, or bathe with herbs like
mugwort, rose, calendula, and jasmine.

MARCH 2024

MONDAY, MARCH 25
Full Moon ○ ♎ 3:00 AM EDT
Penumbral Lunar Eclipse 3:12 AM EDT

TUESDAY, MARCH 26
► Moon void of course begins 7:09 PM EDT

WEDNESDAY, MARCH 27
Moon enters Scorpio ♏ 5:03 AM EDT

THURSDAY, MARCH 28

FRIDAY, MARCH 29
► Moon void of course begins 11:40 AM EDT
Moon enters Sagittarius ♐ 3:52 PM EDT

SATURDAY, MARCH 30

SUNDAY, MARCH 31
► Moon void of course begins 8:16 PM EDT

- Lily of the Valley -
Lifting Your Spirits

Work with clary sage and owl energy to awaken the wisdom of your subconscious.

THIS MONTH:

Mercury Retrograde: April 1-25
New Moon in Aries: April 8
Total Solar Eclipse: April 8
Sun enters Taurus: April 19
Full Moon in Scorpio: April 23

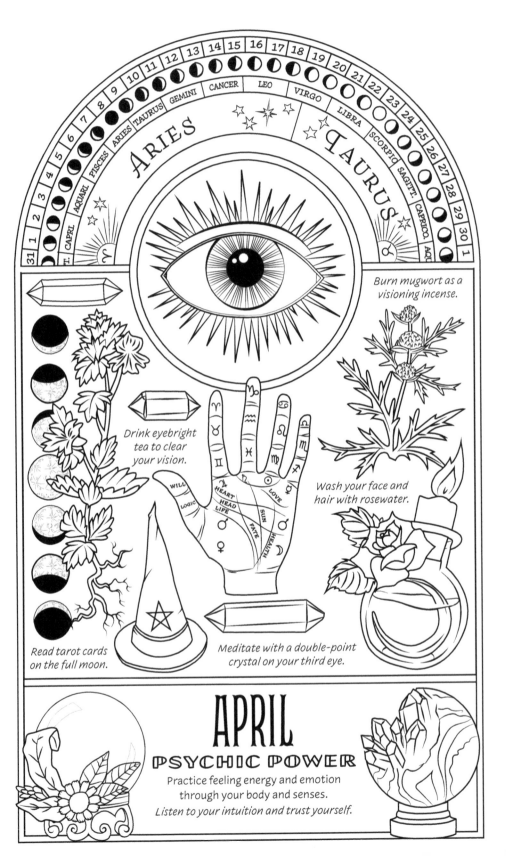

Burn mugwort as a visioning incense.

Drink eyebright tea to clear your vision.

Wash your face and hair with rosewater.

Read tarot cards on the full moon.

Meditate with a double-point crystal on your third eye.

APRIL

PSYCHIC POWER

Practice feeling energy and emotion
through your body and senses.
Listen to your intuition and trust yourself.

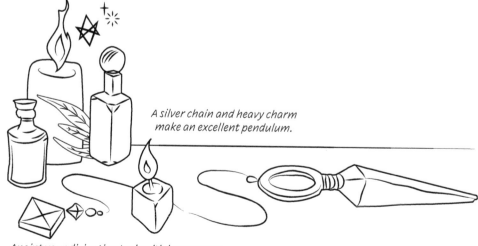

A silver chain and heavy charm make an excellent pendulum.

Anoint your divination tools with lemongrass oil to increase their psychic energy.

MIRROR OF THE MIND
PSYCHIC DEVELOPMENT

Everything has an energy or a "vibe," and "psychic power" is the ability to sense energy within yourself and outside of yourself. Psychic power is a pillar of magic, so practice often and see what happens when you trust your intuition.

THE STAIRCASE: A classic! Descend stairs in your mind's eye as you count down from ten to one (or try visualizing the spectrum of colors).

You'll find yourself in your subconscious mind or magic workshop. In that space, you can access your intuition and deepen your intentions.

TO SHARPEN YOUR SENSES: Ask yourself:

ENERGETIC SELF: What am I feeling in my gut? In my body? How does that compare to my thoughts? What am I sensing? What are my emotions? What is my vibe?

ENERGETICS OF OTHERS: Practice feeling or seeing the energy of other people, animals, plants, and objects. You might like to journey inside a crystal or plant in your mind's eye.

PHYSICAL SENSES: Touch different surfaces and notice their temperature. Try new spices and herbs, either by smelling or tasting. Look closely at shadows and light, and notice how light changes the color and mood of objects.

WORK WITH YOUR THOUGHTS: You can't control your thoughts, but you can work with them. Say/think, "I'm going to move my attention now," when you come across unwanted thoughts.

WORK WITH YOUR EMOTIONS: Feel the heck out of your emotions, even if they hurt. Name them out loud. Say where they are in your body and what they feel like. Then practice shifting to a different energy that you would prefer to feel.

APRIL 2024

	SUNDAY	MONDAY	TUESDAY
	31	1 Last Quarter ◑	2
	7	* Total Solar Eclipse 8 New Moon ● ♈	9
	14	15 First Quarter ◐	16
	21	22	23 Full Moon ○ ♏
	28	29	30

Violet

INTENTIONS
Trust Your Intuition.

Aquamarine

WEDNESDAY	THURSDAY	FRIDAY	SATURDAY
3	4	5	6
10	11	12	13
		☉ Sun enters Taurus	
17	18	19	20
24	25	26	27
★ Beltane (Fixed Date)			★ Beltane 8:11 PM EDT
1 Last Quarter ◑	2	3	4

APRIL 2024

MONDAY, APRIL 1
Moon enters Capricorn ♑ 12:05 AM EDT
Last Quarter ◑ 11:15 PM EDT
☿℞ Mercury Retrograde begins (ends April 25)

TUESDAY, APRIL 2

WEDNESDAY, APRIL 3
► Moon void of course begins 1:40 AM EDT
Moon enters Aquarius ♒ 5:08 AM EDT

THURSDAY, APRIL 4

FRIDAY, APRIL 5
► Moon void of course begins 1:39 AM EDT
Moon enters Pisces ♓ 7:13 AM EDT

SATURDAY, APRIL 6

SUNDAY, APRIL 7
► Moon void of course begins 4:27 AM EDT
Moon enters Aries ♈ 7:25 AM EDT

*Work with basil and amethyst
to clear your aura and space.*

APRIL 2024

MONDAY, APRIL 8
☉ Total Solar Eclipse 2:17 PM EDT
New Moon ● ♈ 2:21 PM EDT
► Moon void of course begins 10:39 PM EDT

TUESDAY, APRIL 9
Moon enters Taurus ♉ 7:23 AM EDT

WEDNESDAY, APRIL 10

THURSDAY, APRIL 11
► Moon void of course begins 6:04 AM EDT
Moon enters Gemini ♊ 8:58 AM EDT

FRIDAY, APRIL 12

SATURDAY, APRIL 13
► Moon void of course begins 10:46 AM EDT
Moon enters Cancer ♋ 1:45 AM EDT

SUNDAY, APRIL 14

OWL

*Channel owl energy
to glean wisdom
from a higher
power.*

APRIL 2024

MONDAY, APRIL 15
First Quarter ◐ 3:15 PM EDT
► Moon void of course begins 7:22 PM EDT

TUESDAY, APRIL 16
Moon enters Leo ♌ 10:24 PM EDT

WEDNESDAY, APRIL 17

THURSDAY, APRIL 18
► Moon void of course begins 8:02 AM EDT
Moon enters Virgo ♍ 10:10 AM EDT

FRIDAY, APRIL 19
☉ Sun enters Taurus ♉ 9:59 AM EDT

SATURDAY, APRIL 20
► Moon void of course begins 8:20 PM EDT
Moon enters Virgo ♍ 11:08 PM EDT

SUNDAY, APRIL 21

To amplify intuitive dreams, place
a sachet of rose petals, amethyst,
and silver under your pillow.

APRIL 2024

MONDAY, APRIL 22
▶ Moon void of course begins 7:24 PM EDT

TUESDAY, APRIL 23
Moon enters Scorpio ♏ 11:20 AM EDT
Full Moon ○ ♏ 7:49 PM EDT

WEDNESDAY, APRIL 24

THURSDAY, APRIL 25
▶ Moon void of course begins 7:17 PM EDT
Moon enters Sagittarius ♐ 9:37 PM EDT
☿℞ Mercury Retrograde ends

FRIDAY, APRIL 26

SATURDAY, APRIL 27

SUNDAY, APRIL 28
▶ Moon void of course begins 3:31 AM EDT
Moon enters Capricorn ♑ 5:37 AM EDT

*Strengthen your psychic abilities
with horehound tea or mint candy.*

APRIL/MAY 2024

MONDAY, APRIL 29

TUESDAY, APRIL 30
► Moon void of course begins 11:19 AM EDT
Moon enters Aquarius ♒ 11:20 AM EDT

WEDNESDAY, MAY 1
★ Beltane (Fixed Festival Date)
Last Quarter ☽ 7:27 AM EDT

Mugwort

THURSDAY, MAY 2
► Moon void of course begins 5:28 AM EDT
Moon enters Pisces ♓ 2:52 PM EDT
℞ Pluto Retrograde begins (ends Oct. 11)

Elderflowers

FRIDAY, MAY 3

Violets

SATURDAY, MAY 4
★ Beltane (Astronomical Date) 8:11 PM EST
► Moon void of course begins 3:06 PM EDT
Moon enters Aries ♈ 4:41 PM EDT

SUNDAY, MAY 5

BELTANE
Feel magical energy growing with your intentions.
Cast flowers into a fire or body of water as you
make a wish for something wonderful.

WITCH'S HAT

Amplify your psychic powers with calendula, cinnamon, or rose.

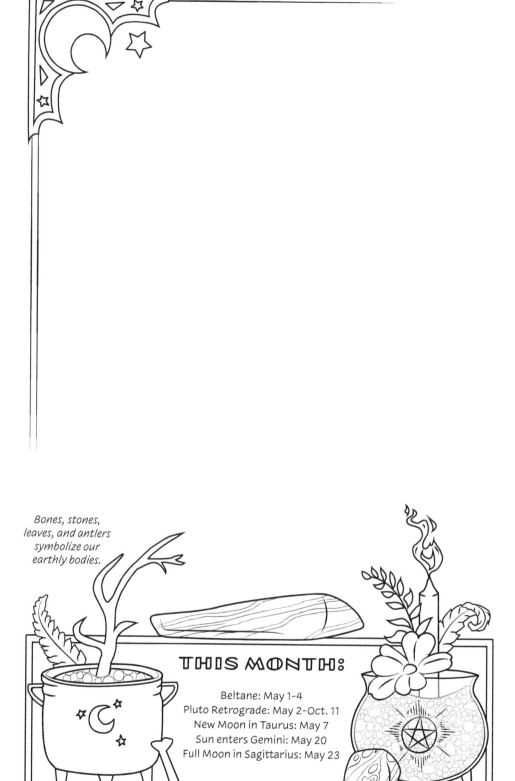

Bones, stones, leaves, and antlers symbolize our earthly bodies.

THIS MONTH:

Beltane: May 1-4
Pluto Retrograde: May 2-Oct. 11
New Moon in Taurus: May 7
Sun enters Gemini: May 20
Full Moon in Sagittarius: May 23

-Earth-
The Element
of Stability

Grow plants to
feel the magic
of the earth.

Ground yourself
with smoky
quartz.

Grind grains and herbs to
connect with their energy.

Place mandrake root with
coins to increase abundance.

MAY
POWER OF EARTH
Spend time grounding and aligning with the
energy of plants, animals, and nature.
Perform spells to improve your living space.

Wishing Stones have a single unbroken stripe. Make a wish, then bury the stone or throw it into a body of water. Hagstones have holes in them. Nail a hagstone over your door for protection.

Primrose will protect your garden and attract fairies and love.

ELEMENT OF EARTH
ROCK-SOLID SUPPORT FOR YOUR MAGIC

The earth element carries a feeling of belonging, stability, and peace. You "belong" to the Earth as a creature of this planet, and therefore you have a place and purpose. You are capable, secure, meant to be here, and supported in this physical realm.

Earth also represents the cycles of life and death, and the polarity between them—you can't have one without the other.

SIMPLE EARTH SPELLS: The Earth grows new life and also eventually disintegrates it. To use these powers in a spell, bury an herb or a small stone or crystal with the intention of either "to grow" or "to bury" what you wish to let go of. Imagine or feel the energy of what you wish to grow sprouting like a seed, and what you intend to release disintegrating back into the Earth.

Another classic is to plant a seed (or garden) as you set an intention. As you tend to your plant(s), reconnect to your intentions and ground into the energy of what you desire as if it already exists in the physical realm on earth.

CONNECTING WITH EARTH ENERGY:

The simplest way is to just experience nature until you feel your energy shift (you'll know!), or to hold a plant, rock or crystal in your hand and focus on its energy and vibration in your body.

You can also imagine yourself here on Earth, first growing roots, then becoming a giant tree. Grow in your mind's eye until you are viewing the entire planet. Sit with that till your energy shifts, then shrink back into yourself.

And of course, you can use earthy ingredients and energy in any of your spells and rituals.

MAY 2024

	SUNDAY	MONDAY	TUESDAY
	28	29	30
	5	6	7 New Moon ● ♉
	12	13	14
	19	20 ☉ Sun enters Gemini ♊	21
	26	27	28

INTENTIONS
Ground Yourself.

-Mushrooms and Ferns-
The Magic of the Forest

WEDNESDAY	THURSDAY	FRIDAY	SATURDAY
★ Beltane (Fixed Date) 1 Last Quarter ◑	2	3	★ Beltane 8:11 PM EDT 4
8	9	10	11
15 First Quarter ◑	16	17	18
22	23 Full Moon ○ ♐	24	25
29	30 Last Quarter ◑	31	1

MAY 2024

MONDAY, MAY 6
▸ Moon void of course begins 1:57 AM EDT
Moon enters Taurus ♉ 5:42 PM EDT

TUESDAY, MAY 7
New Moon ● ♉ 11:22 PM EDT

WEDNESDAY, MAY 8
▸ Moon void of course begins 5:55 PM EDT
Moon enters Gemini ♊ 7:20 PM EDT

THURSDAY, MAY 9

FRIDAY, MAY 10
▸ Moon void of course begins 9:49 PM EDT
Moon enters Cancer ♋ 11:13 PM EDT

SATURDAY, MAY 11

SUNDAY, MAY 12

*Sweep in the energy of
abundance with a broom made
from wheat straw or vervain.*

MAY 2024

MONDAY, MAY 13
► Moon void of course 5:13 AM EDT
Moon enters Leo ♌ 6:36 AM EDT

TUESDAY, MAY 14

WEDNESDAY, MAY 15
First Quarter ◐ 7:48 AM EDT
► Moon void of course begins 12:41 PM EDT
Moon enters Virgo ♍ 5:33 PM EDT

THURSDAY, MAY 16

FRIDAY, MAY 17

SATURDAY, MAY 18
► Moon void of course begins 5:09 AM EDT
Moon enters Libra ♎ 6:23 AM EDT

SUNDAY, MAY 19
► Moon void of course begins 11:48 AM EDT

BLACKTHORN

*Powerful protection
from dark energy
and calamity.*

MAY 2024

MONDAY, MAY 20
⊙ Sun enters Gemini ♊ 8:59 AM EDT
Moon enters Scorpio ♏ 6:34 PM EDT

TUESDAY, MAY 21

WEDNESDAY, MAY 22

THURSDAY, MAY 23
► Moon void of course begins 3:28 AM EDT
Moon enters Sagittarius ♐ 4:24 AM EDT
Full Moon ○ ♐ 9:53 AM EDT

FRIDAY, MAY 24

SATURDAY, MAY 25
► Moon void of course begins 10:47 AM EDT
Moon enters Capricorn ♑ 11:36 AM EDT

SUNDAY, MAY 26

*Ground yourself with earthy incense like
patchouli, cypress, or vetivert root.*

MAY/JUNE 2024

MONDAY, MAY 27
▶ Moon void of course begins 4:02 PM EDT
Moon enters Aquarius ♒ 4:45 PM EDT

TUESDAY, MAY 28

WEDNESDAY, MAY 29
▶ Moon void of course begins 10:20 AM EDT
Moon enters Pisces ♓ 8:33 PM EDT

THURSDAY, MAY 30
Last Quarter ◑ 1:13 PM EDT

FRIDAY, MAY 31
▶ Moon void of course begins 10:55 PM EDT
Moon enters Aries ♈ 11:28 PM EDT

SATURDAY, JUNE 1

SUNDAY, JUNE 2
▶ Moon void of course begins 6:04 PM EDT

GOAT

*Gather your focus
and determination
with goat energy.*

Spend a few minutes in the sun,
eyes closed, and absorb its power.

Work with amber
and amber oil.

THIS MONTH:

New Moon in Gemini: June 6
Litha (Summer Solstice): June 20
Sun enters Cancer: June 20
Full Moon in Capricorn: June 21
Saturn Retrograde: June 29-Nov. 15

- Fire -
The Element of
Transformation

Make a powerful wand
with rowan wood.

Watch a
candle burn.

- Phoenix -
Rebirth

Anoint your
broom with
cinnamon oil.

Decorate your home or
altar with amaranth.

JUNE

POWER OF FIRE

Transform yourself through letting go
to make space for something new.
Channel the energy of the Phoenix.

Anoint your candles by rubbing a drop or two of essential oil along the length. Then roll your oiled candle in finely crushed herbs.

Fire Burn
AND
Cauldron Bubble

Witch
Hazel

Oak &
Carnelian

Ametrine

ELEMENT OF FIRE
YOUR POWER TO CHANGE AND CREATE

The fire element is a feeling of rapid transformation, contrasting to earth's stable, steady vibe. Fire is the element of movement, passion, action, and change. It also carries an energy of destruction to rebuild and recreate.

SIMPLE FIRE SPELLS: Candles represent fire and the powerful polarity between light and dark. "Charge" your candles with intention—to bring light to a situation, to amplify the energy of your intentions through the fire, or to "burn something out" if you no longer desire it.

Fire is a powerful element for visioning. Gaze into a flame to connect to intuitive messages. Or wrap a bundle of herbs in a piece of paper or natural fabric and burn it with intention.

CONNECTING WITH FIRE ENERGY:
You don't have to use candles to connect to fire! It's all around us. The sun is a big ball of fire, and so are the stars. You can also use the element of fire in cooking or by connecting to the passion and "fire" within yourself.

Try stargazing, ideally until you see a shooting star, then make a wish. You might also like to fire-gaze into a lightning storm or volcano.

Do things that make you feel "heat" in your body, or practice pranayama "Breath of Fire."

Connect to the sun energy by feeling it on your skin (don't stare at it!).

Watch something burn, or destroy something in order to create something new.

Pretend you are a fire-breathing dragon, or imagine you're shooting flaming arrows into the night sky (do not shoot actual flaming arrows without proper precautions and training).

JUNE 2024

	SUNDAY	MONDAY	TUESDAY
	26	27	28
	2	3	4
	9	10	11
	16	17	18
	23	24	25
	30	1	2

INTENTIONS
Destroy to Create

WEDNESDAY	THURSDAY	FRIDAY	SATURDAY
29	30 Last Quarter ◗	31	1
5	6 New Moon ● ♊	7	8
12	13	14 First Quarter ◐	15
19	20 ★ Litha (Summer Solstice) ☉ Sun enters Cancer ♋	21 Full Moon ○ ♐	22
26	27	28 Last Quarter ◗	29
3	4	5 New Moon ● ♋	6

JUNE 2024

MONDAY, JUNE 3
Moon enters Taurus ♉ 1:55 AM EDT

TUESDAY, JUNE 4

WEDNESDAY, JUNE 5
▸ Moon void of course begins 4:09 AM EDT
Moon enters Gemini ♊ 4:36 AM EDT

THURSDAY, JUNE 6
New Moon ● ♊ 8:38 AM EDT

FRIDAY, JUNE 7
▸ Moon void of course begins 8:16 AM EDT
Moon enters Cancer ♋ 8:41 AM EDT

SATURDAY, JUNE 8

SUNDAY, JUNE 9
▸ Moon void of course begins 3:05 PM EDT
Moon enters Leo ♌ 8:41 AM EDT

*Burn rose geranium,
sweet woodruff, or
star anise to connect
with fire energy.*

JUNE 2024

MONDAY, JUNE 10

TUESDAY, JUNE 11
► Moon void of course begins 3:16 PM EDT

WEDNESDAY, JUNE 12
Moon enters Virgo ♍ 1:39 AM EDT

THURSDAY, JUNE 13

FRIDAY, JUNE 14
First Quarter ◐ 1:18 AM EDT
► Moon void of course begins 1:54 PM EDT
Moon enters Libra ♎ 2:12 PM EDT

SATURDAY, JUNE 15

SUNDAY, JUNE 16

*Feel the energy of
the sun warming
your body.*

JUNE 2024

MONDAY, JUNE 17
► Moon void of course begins 2:05 AM EDT
Moon enters Scorpio ♏ 2:38 AM EDT

TUESDAY, JUNE 18

WEDNESDAY, JUNE 19
► Moon void of course begins 2:05 AM EDT
Moon enters Sagittarius ♐ 12:32 PM EDT

THURSDAY, JUNE 20
★ Litha (Summer Solstice) 4:51 PM EDT
☉ Sun enters Cancer ♋ 4:51 PM EDT

FRIDAY, JUNE 21
► Moon void of course begins 6:58 PM
Moon enters Capricorn ♑ 7:08 PM EDT
Full Moon ○ ♑ 9:08 PM EDT

SATURDAY, JUNE 22

SUNDAY, JUNE 23
► Moon void of course begins 11:05 PM EDT
Moon enters Aquarius ♒ 11:14 PM EDT

Sweet Woodruff

LITHA

Feel the magic of the sun. Remember that you can change, grow, and live a bright life by working with herbs like cinquefoil, woodruff, and cinnamon.

JUNE 2024

MONDAY, JUNE 24

TUESDAY, JUNE 25
► Moon void of course begins 6:30 PM EDT
Moon enters Pisces ♓ 2:08 AM EDT

WEDNESDAY, JUNE 26

THURSDAY, JUNE 27

FRIDAY, JUNE 28
► Moon void of course begins 4:45 AM EDT
Moon enters Aries ♈ 4:52 AM EDT
Last Quarter ☽ 5:53 PM EDT

SATURDAY, JUNE 29
♄℞ Saturn Retrograde begins (ends November 15)

SUNDAY, JUNE 30
► Moon void of course begins 12:56 AM EDT
Moon enters Taurus ♉ 8:00 AM EDT

*Hang St. John's Wort over your
door or place it on your altar to
bring happiness to your home.*

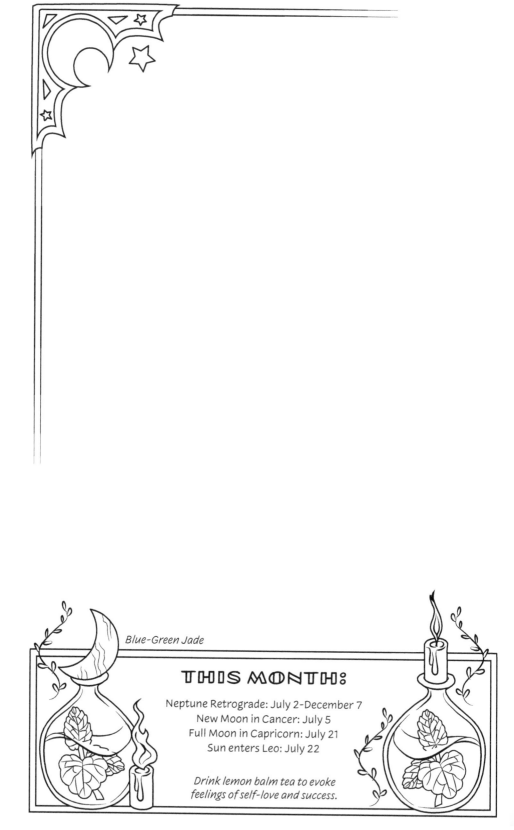

Blue-Green Jade

THIS MONTH:

Neptune Retrograde: July 2–December 7
New Moon in Cancer: July 5
Full Moon in Capricorn: July 21
Sun enters Leo: July 22

*Drink lemon balm tea to evoke
feelings of self-love and success.*

- Water -
The Element of
Emotions

- Aquamarine -
Calming your
thoughts

- Willow-
Moon and
Witch Power

Bathe with eucalyptus to
clarify emotions or with
skullcap for inner peace.

Wash your hair
with jasmine and
rose water.

JULY
POWER OF WATER
Flow with the ups and downs of life as you
follow your intuition and hold your intentions.
Walk along the seashore or near a river or creek.

Make moon water with sea salt, orchids, or lavender to release stagnant emotional patterns and clear your intuition. Then welcome new energy.

Turquoise

Aloe

Orris Root

FLOW.

ELEMENT OF WATER
THE LANGUAGE OF YOUR EMOTIONS

The water element embodies the power of emotions, intuition, and the wisdom of the subconscious mind. It also represents clearing, washing, releasing, and letting go.

SIMPLE WATER SPELLS: Use the power of water by washing, bathing, or swimming while releasing energy and feeling your intentions.

Try glinting the moon's light off a vessel or a body of water while gazing at its reflection. Or look for shapes that form as the moon dances off the waves or watery ripples.

Classic water spells include blessing yourself in a body of water or tossing herbs or rocks into water while you cast an intention. Pouring or sprinkling water over something to bless it is also a timeless spell, as is making moon waters, baths, floor washes, and blessing waters.

CONNECTING WITH WATER ENERGY:

Submerge yourself in a bath or natural body of water, or pour spring water over your head. Imagine you are the water flowing down a riverbed, or building and releasing in cycles of waves when you face difficult situations.

SOUL BATH: Water is the element of dreams and emotions, and you can use it to listen to the wisdom that exists right now, deep in your soul. Mix 1/2 cup of sea salt and 1/4 cup of dried herbs and petals (like mugwort, jasmine, rose, and lavender). Sprinkle the mix into your bath, or fill a sachet with herbs and tie it under your shower head. Allow yourself to slip into the space between worlds, and ask for the quiet voice of guidance to rise to the surface. Listen closely! Your intuitive voice is subtle and gentle.

JULY 2024

	SUNDAY	MONDAY	TUESDAY
	30	1	2
	7	8	9
	14	15	16
	21 Full Moon ○ ♑	☉ Sun enters Leo ♌ 22	23
	28	29	30

INTENTIONS
Go with the Flow.

Gardenia & Moonstone

WEDNESDAY	THURSDAY	FRIDAY	SATURDAY
3	4	5 New Moon ● ♋	6
10	11	12	13 First Quarter ◐
17	18	19	20
24	25	26	27 Last Quarter ◑
31	★ Lughnasadh (Fixed Date) 1	2	3

JULY 2024

MONDAY, JULY 1

TUESDAY, JULY 2
► Moon void of course begins 11:43 AM EDT
Moon enters Gemini ♊ 11:50 AM EDT
♆℞ Neptune Retrograde begins (ends December 7)

WEDNESDAY, JULY 3

THURSDAY, JULY 4
► Moon void of course begins 4:44 PM EDT
Moon enters Cancer ♋ 4:51 PM EDT

FRIDAY, JULY 5
New Moon ● ♋ 6:57 PM EDT

SATURDAY, JULY 6
► Moon void of course begins 11:47 PM EDT
Moon enters Leo ♌ 11:56 PM EDT

SUNDAY, JULY 7

*Feel calming energies with larimar,
valerian root, and chamomile.*

JULY 2024

MONDAY, JULY 8

TUESDAY, JULY 9
► Moon void of course begins 2:04 AM EDT
Moon enters Virgo ♍ 9:47 AM EDT

WEDNESDAY, JULY 10

THURSDAY, JULY 11
► Moon void of course begins 9:55 PM EDT
Moon enters Libra ♎ 10:06 PM EDT

FRIDAY, JULY 12

SATURDAY, JULY 13
► Moon void of course begins 6:49 PM EDT
First Quarter ◑ 6:49 PM EDT

SUNDAY, JULY 14
Moon enters Scorpio ♏ 10:53 AM EDT

FROG

Transform in magical ways with frog energy.

JULY 2024

MONDAY, JULY 15

TUESDAY, JULY 16
► Moon void of course begins 9:10 PM EDT
Moon enters Sagittarius ♐ 9:25 PM EDT

WEDNESDAY, JULY 17

THURSDAY, JULY 18

FRIDAY, JULY 19
► Moon void of course begins 3:58 AM EDT
Moon enters Capricorn ♑ 4:14 AM EDT

SATURDAY, JULY 20

SUNDAY, JULY 21
Full Moon ○ ♑ 6:17 AM EDT
► Moon void of course begins 7:26 AM EDT
Moon enters Aquarius ♒ 7:43 AM EDT

Make an elemental floor wash with sprigs of thyme (water), lavender (air), cloves (fire), and vetivert (earth).

JULY 2024

MONDAY, JULY 22
☉ Sun enters Leo ♌ 3:44 AM EDT

TUESDAY, JULY 23
► Moon void of course begins 5:56 AM EDT
Moon enters Pisces ♓ 9:23 AM EDT

WEDNESDAY, JULY 24

THURSDAY, JULY 25
► Moon void of course begins 10:31 AM EDT
Moon enters Aries ♈ 10:52 AM EDT

FRIDAY, JULY 26
► Moon void of course begins 6:14 PM EDT

SATURDAY, JULY 27
Moon enters Taurus ♉ 1:23 PM EDT
Last Quarter ☽ 10:52 PM EDT

SUNDAY, JULY 28

CORNFLOWER

The energy of the moon and changing tides of life.

JULY/AUGUST 2024

MONDAY, JULY 29
➤ Moon void of course begins 4:59 PM EDT
Moon enters Gemini ♊ 5:28 PM EDT

TUESDAY, JULY 30

WEDNESDAY, JULY 31
➤ Moon void of course begins 10:46 PM EDT
Moon enters Cancer ♋ 11:19 PM EDT

THURSDAY, AUGUST 1
★ Lughnasadh (Fixed Festival Date)

FRIDAY, AUGUST 2

SATURDAY, AUGUST 3
➤ Moon void of course begins 6:31 AM EDT
Moon enters Leo ♌ 7:10 AM EDT

SUNDAY, AUGUST 4
New Moon ● ♌ 7:13 AM EDT

LUGHNASADH

Feel the magic of gratitude. Harvest berries or herbs, or bake, eat, and enjoy an abundance of these things in a ritual meal.

- Blackberry -
Protection and Nourishment

Make a wish as you blow the seeds off a dandelion puff.

THIS MONTH:

Lughnasadh: August 1-6
Mercury Retrograde: August 5-28
New Moon in Leo: August 4
Sun enters Virgo: August 22
Full Moon in Aquarius: August 19

31 1 2 3 4 5 6 7 8 9 10 11 12 13 14 15 16 17 18 19 20 21 22 23 24 25 26 27 28 29 30 31
CANCER
LEO
VIRGO
LIBRA
SCORPIO
SAGITT.
CAPRICO.
AQUA.
PISCES
ARIES
TAURUS
GEMINI
CANCER
LEO
VIRGO
- Air -
The Element
of Ideas
Swing a hagstone
on a string to
regain witch
power.
Ring
bells for
protective
magic.
Finding a raven's
feather is a sign of
witch power.
Hang keys or spoons as
wind chimes to stir up or
unlock opportunities.
AUGUST
POWER OF AIR
Use your voice by chanting, singing, playing
music, or expressing yourself through art.
Express thoughts or feelings that've been on your mind.

Watch steam rise off a cup of dandelion tea as you go to sleep. Take a sip of the cold tea in the morning to enhance dream recall and intuitive messages.

Air Above

Burn acacia wood as you speak your wishes and intentions out loud.

Element of Air
The Magic of Self-Expression and Voice

Air symbolizes the power of knowing, in contrast to water's feelings and emotions. Air is the power of your breath and voice (self-expression). Your voice is a powerful force of change and influence in the world, so use it!

The wisdom of air is always flowing through you in your breath. Breath is life, magic, and universal wisdom moving through you at all times.

SIMPLE AIR SPELLS: Air moves energy and magic to you, through you, or away from you, depending on your intention.

Classic "air" spells involve tossing herbs off of a cliff, or tying ribbons to trees that represent wishes, and letting them blow in the breeze. Try casting your spells in a windstorm to increase their energy. You might like to stab the air with a knife (careful, now!) or wildly snip scissors as

you speak what you wish to release, such as an energy within yourself or ties with other people.

Use a broom and the power of air to sweep intentions "in" to your door (or clockwise), or sweep "out" (or counterclockwise) to release.

Windows are portals of air's magic. Paint sigils and symbols on your windows, use sun catchers, or place herbs, plants, charms, and crystals on your sills to blow magic inside with the wind.

CONNECTING WITH AIR ENERGY: Find a quiet place to listen to your own breath, or speak things that wish to be spoken, either aloud or through writing or art.

And to receive powerful "air" wisdom, find a good windy spot outdoors and ask the spirit of air to talk to you or provide guidance. Feel and listen closely as the wind blows.

AUGUST 2024

	SUNDAY	MONDAY	TUESDAY
	28	29	30
			★ Lughnasadh 8:10 PM EDT
	4 New Moon ● ♌	5	6
	11	12 First Quarter ◑	13
	18	19 Full Moon ○ ♒	20
	25	26 Last Quarter ◑	27

INTENTIONS

Express Yourself.

- Chicory -
Ease

- Blue Lace Agate -
Peaceful Self-Expression

WEDNESDAY	THURSDAY	FRIDAY	SATURDAY
31	★ Lughnasadh (Fixed Date) 1	2	3
7	8	9	10
14	15	16	17
21	☉ Sun enters Virgo ♍ 22	23	24
28	29	30	31

AUGUST 2024

MONDAY, AUGUST 5
► Moon void of course begins 11:16 AM EDT
Moon enters Virgo ♍ 5:17 PM EDT
☿℞ Mercury Retrograde begins (ends August 28)

TUESDAY, AUGUST 6
★ Lughnasadh (Astronomical Date) 8:10 PM EDT

WEDNESDAY, AUGUST 7

THURSDAY, AUGUST 8
► Moon void of course begins 4:40 PM EDT
Moon enters Libra ♎ 5:31 AM EDT

FRIDAY, AUGUST 9
► Moon void of course begins 5:45 PM EDT

SATURDAY, AUGUST 10
Moon enters Scorpio ♏ 6:34 PM EDT

SUNDAY, AUGUST 11

*If you find a raven's feather,
wear it in your hat for energetic
protection and witch power.*

AUGUST 2024

MONDAY, AUGUST 12
First Quarter ◑ 11:19 AM EDT

TUESDAY, AUGUST 13
▸ Moon void of course begins 5:01 AM EDT
Moon enters Sagittarius ♐ 6:01 AM EDT

WEDNESDAY, AUGUST 14

THURSDAY, AUGUST 15
▸ Moon void of course begins 12:52 PM EDT
Moon enters Capricorn ♑ 1:51 PM EDT

FRIDAY, AUGUST 16

SATURDAY, AUGUST 17
▸ Moon void of course begins 4:43 PM EDT
Moon enters Aquarius ♒ 5:45 PM EDT

SUNDAY, AUGUST 18

RAVEN

Channel raven energy to speak from your heart.

AUGUST 2024

MONDAY, AUGUST 19
► Moon void of course begins 2:26 PM EDT
Full Moon ○ ≈ 2:26 PM EDT
Moon enters Pisces ♓ 6:52 PM EDT

TUESDAY, AUGUST 20

WEDNESDAY, AUGUST 21
► Moon void of course begins 5:54 PM EDT
Moon enters Aries ♈ 7:02 PM EDT

THURSDAY, AUGUST 22
☉ Sun enters Virgo ♍ 10:54 AM EDT

FRIDAY, AUGUST 23
► Moon void of course begins 8:44 AM EDT
Moon enters Taurus ♉ 8:00 PM EDT

SATURDAY, AUGUST 24

SUNDAY, AUGUST 25
► Moon void of course begins 9:40 PM EDT
Moon enters Gemini ♊ 11:04 PM EDT

*Plant a window box with herbs that signify
your intentions. Open the window and let
the breeze blow magic into your house.*

AUGUST/SEPTEMBER 2024

MONDAY, AUGUST 26
Last Quarter ☾ 5:26 AM EDT

TUESDAY, AUGUST 27

WEDNESDAY, AUGUST 28
► Moon void of course begins 3:14 AM EDT
Moon enters Cancer ♋ 4:47 AM EDT
☿℞ Mercury Retrograde ends

THURSDAY, AUGUST 29

FRIDAY, AUGUST 30
► Moon void of course begins 11:24 AM EDT
Moon enters Leo ♌ 1:09 AM EDT

SATURDAY, AUGUST 31

SUNDAY, SEPTEMBER 1
► Moon void of course begins 8:25 PM EDT
Moon enters Virgo ♍ 11:48 PM EDT
♅℞ Uranus Retrograde begins (ends Jan. 30, 2025)

SCISSORS

Cut fresh herbs (like mint) to help you make decisions.

THIS MONTH:

Uranus Retrograde: September 1 -Jan. 30, 2025
New Moon in Virgo: September 2
Full Moon in Pisces: September 17
Partial Lunar Eclipse: September 17
Sun enters Libra: September 22
Mabon (Autumnal Equinox): September 22

- Pentacle -
The Laws of Magic

-Herkimer
Diamond-
Attuning
to Spirit

Fly beyond your
limitations.

Consecrate your robe &
hat with magical scents.

Follow your curiosity &
desires of your spirit.

SEPTEMBER
POWER OF SPIRIT
Reconnect to the experiences, rituals, and everyday
things that make you feel magical.
Listen closely to your intuition and follow it.

Weaving the Web
Create Your Signature Spell

By now you're familiar with the magic of the four elements (earth, fire, air, and water). Many witches believe that the fifth point of the pentagram represents the fifth element—SPIRIT.

So how do you connect with spirit or perform a spell of spirit?! This is personal and unique to you. Spirit is the magic that only you can do, and you don't need a written spell to do it.

WHAT IS SACRED TO YOU? What scents, sights, sounds, and mechanisms evoke magic within you? Is it all within your mind and energetic body? Or do you use herbs, candles, or representations of the four physical elements? Give it a feel and then write it down. There is no right and wrong here. Just search for the things that make you *feel the magic* within.

You might like to pick one tool that you keep constant throughout your work (like a cauldron, wand, crystal, figurine, broom, hat, or robe).

It's also helpful to pick one signature scent (an incense or oil) that you use only for magic, so when you smell it, you'll be automatically moved to the feeling of spirit and magic within.

CREATE YOUR SIGNATURE SPELL: This will be a spell that you know intuitively, so you can do it anytime for any intention. It can be simple, but that's up to you. Use this example as a starting point or create something entirely unique.

Carve your name, a deity's name, or a symbol into a candle. Light the candle and a cauldron of incense. Cast a circle, moving until you feel your energy shift. Sit in the circle. Chant until you feel a tingly sense of magic within. Speak your intention, then listen for intuitive wisdom.

SEPTEMBER 2024

SUNDAY	MONDAY	TUESDAY
1	2 New Moon ● ♍	3
8	9	10
15	16	★Partial Lunar Eclipse 17 Full Moon ○ ♓
☉ Sun enters Libra ♎ ★ Mabon (Autumnal Equinox) 22	23	24 Last Quarter ◑
29	30	1

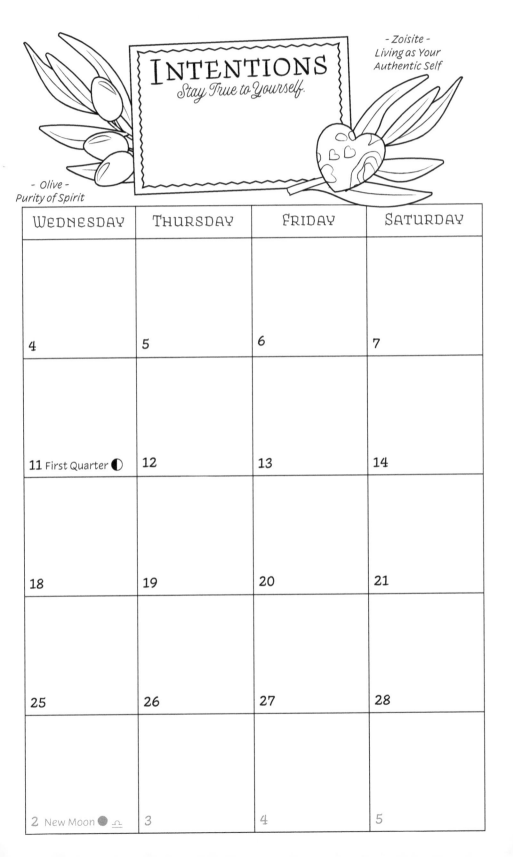

INTENTIONS
Stay True to Yourself.

- Olive -
Purity of Spirit

WEDNESDAY	THURSDAY	FRIDAY	SATURDAY
4	5	6	7
11 First Quarter ◑	12	13	14
18	19	20	21
25	26	27	28
2 New Moon ● ♎	3	4	5

SEPTEMBER 2024

MONDAY, SEPTEMBER 2
New Moon ● ♍ 9:56 PM EDT

TUESDAY, SEPTEMBER 3

WEDNESDAY, SEPTEMBER 4
► Moon void of course begins 12:06 PM EDT
Moon enters Libra ♎ 12:12 PM EDT

THURSDAY, SEPTEMBER 5

FRIDAY, SEPTEMBER 6

SATURDAY, SEPTEMBER 7
► Moon void of course begins 1:08 AM EDT
Moon enters Scorpio ♏ 1:18 AM EDT

SUNDAY, SEPTEMBER 8

Use your favorite sacred herb or incense in your rituals to associate that scent with magic and amplify its suggestive power.

SEPTEMBER 2024

MONDAY, SEPTEMBER 9
► Moon void of course begins 1:11 PM EDT
Moon enters Sagittarius ♐ 1:26 PM EDT

TUESDAY, SEPTEMBER 10

WEDNESDAY, SEPTEMBER 11
First Quarter ☽ 2:06 AM EDT
► Moon void of course begins 8:21 PM EDT
Moon enters Capricorn ♑ 10:38 PM EDT

THURSDAY, SEPTEMBER 12

FRIDAY, SEPTEMBER 13

SATURDAY, SEPTEMBER 14
► Moon void of course begins 3:35 AM EDT
Moon enters Aquarius ♒ 3:53 AM EDT

SUNDAY, SEPTEMBER 15

THE VEIL

What does "spirit"
mean to you?
When do you feel
spiritual?

SEPTEMBER 2024

MONDAY, SEPTEMBER 16
► Moon void of course begins 1:04 AM EDT
Moon enters Pisces ♓ 5:39 AM EDT

TUESDAY, SEPTEMBER 17
Full Moon ○ ♓ 10:34 PM EDT
Partial Lunar Eclipse 10:44 PM EDT

WEDNESDAY, SEPTEMBER 18
► Moon void of course begins 5:02 AM EDT
Moon enters Aries ♈ 5:24 AM EDT

THURSDAY, SEPTEMBER 19

FRIDAY, SEPTEMBER 20
► Moon void of course begins 4:39 AM EDT
Moon enters Taurus ♉ 5:03 AM EDT

SATURDAY, SEPTEMBER 21

SUNDAY, SEPTEMBER 22
☉ Sun enters Libra ♎ 8:43 AM EDT
★ Mabon (Autumnal Equinox) 8:43 AM EDT

MABON

*Feel the magic of release. Courageously follow
your intuition towards what you desire, and
allow yourself to slowly let go of the rest.*

SEPTEMBER 2024

MONDAY, SEPTEMBER 23

TUESDAY, SEPTEMBER 24
► Moon void of course begins 7:59 AM EDT
Moon enters Cancer ♋ 10:50 AM EDT
Last Quarter ◑ 2:50 PM EST

WEDNESDAY, SEPTEMBER 25

THURSDAY, SEPTEMBER 26
► Moon void of course begins 6:12 PM EDT
Moon enters Leo ♌ 6:47 PM EDT

FRIDAY, SEPTEMBER 27

SATURDAY, SEPTEMBER 28
► Moon void of course begins 11:36 PM EDT

SUNDAY, SEPTEMBER 29
Moon enters Virgo ♍ 5:42 AM EDT

*Burn apple wood or enjoy the
taste of apples to remind you
of the immortality of spirit.*

SEPTEMBER/OCTOBER 2024

MONDAY, SEPTEMBER 30

TUESDAY, OCTOBER 1
► Moon void of course begins 5:39 PM EDT
Moon enters Libra ♎ 6:20 PM EDT

WEDNESDAY, OCTOBER 2
New Moon ● ♎ 2:49 PM EDT
Annular Solar Eclipse 2:44 PM EDT

THURSDAY, OCTOBER 3

FRIDAY, OCTOBER 4
► Moon void of course begins 6:40 AM EDT
Moon enters Scorpio ♏ 7:22 AM EDT

SATURDAY, OCTOBER 5

SUNDAY, OCTOBER 6
► Moon void of course begins 10:52 AM EDT
Moon enters Sagittarius ♐ 7:34 PM EDT

- Kyanite & Clary Sage -
Connection to Spirit Guides

FLIGHT

*Trust yourself and
follow your spirit.*

Place statues of toads or gargoyles to protect your home and garden.

THIS MONTH:

New Moon in Libra: October 2
Annular Solar Eclipse: October 2
Jupiter ℞: Oct. 9-Feb. 4, 2025
Pluto ℞ ends: October 11
Full Moon in Aries: October 17
Sun enters Scorpio: October 22
Samhain: Oct. 31- Nov. 6

Interlocking patterns are protective.

- Magic Knot-
Elemental Protection

Yarrow

Nails signify protection.

- Witch Bottles -
A classic!

White candles protect your magic.

Burdock Root

Enchant a lock and key.

Set protective charms at doors, windows, & thresholds.

OCTOBER
PROTECTION

Create a sacred space where you feel safe, secure, and surrounded by your magic.
Cast a perimeter spell around your home.

Burn angelica or
hang a bundle over
your door.

Seal jars, spells, and
scrolls with wax.

Make a ring around
your home with iron,
salt, and silver.

... And vinegar.

Place black tourmaline at
the corners of your house.

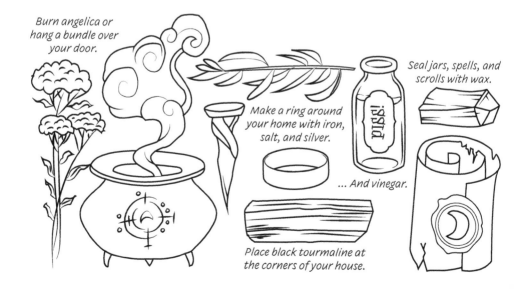

IN THIS CIRCLE...

Place bay leaves at the four corners of your home.

Design your own protection sigil and draw it in this shield.

NO HARM SHALL PASS.

PROTECTION SPELLS
CREATE AN ENERGETIC SHIELD

A shield or protection spell is an energetic boundary. Shields create a magical space where you decide what may enter, and what may not.

The purpose of "casting a circle" in spellcraft is to create a container for your magic spell and also to form a protective shield. Circles, interlocking shapes, and symbols made of unbroken lines (like the pentagram) are ancient mechanisms of energetic protection.

PROTECTION AND SHIELDING SPELLS:

The "classic" energetic shield involves creating a bubble of light or an "egg" around you where no harm shall pass. Imagine the "vibes" and things you do not wish to reach you bouncing off the outside of the shield. Decide what your boundaries are and adhere to them. You might like to refresh your shield each day.

If you do run into an energy outside of your boundary, (events, conversations, trains of thought, etc.) try your best to not engage. Put up your shield and re-set that energetic line.

There are endless ways to use physical magic and amulets for protection, too. Charge a piece of jewelry, crystal, or amulet that you carry with you. Or create a charm to hang in your home—a pentacle over your door, salt sprinkled at the four corners, or a bundle of herbs will help to dissipate or "send back" whatever energy you do not wish to enter your space.

You might try placing statues or symbols of gargoyles, dragons, or other fierce creatures and charge them with your protective intentions.

And carry an aura of confidence and power with you wherever you go. You are a witch!

OCTOBER 2024

	SUNDAY	MONDAY	TUESDAY
	29	30	1
	6	7	8
	13	14	15
	20	21	22 ⊙ Sun enters Scorpio
	27	28	29

Jet & Onyx

INTENTIONS
Protect Your Energy.

Heather, Bay,
& Rosemary

WEDNESDAY	THURSDAY	FRIDAY	SATURDAY
★Annular Solar Eclipse 2 New Moon ● ♎	3	4	5
9	10 First Quarter ◐	11	12
16	17 Full Moon ○ ♈	18	19
23	24 Last Quarter ◑	25	26
30	★Samhain (fixed date) 31	1 New Moon ● ♏	2

OCTOBER 2024

MONDAY, OCTOBER 7

TUESDAY, OCTOBER 8

WEDNESDAY, OCTOBER 9
➤ Moon void of course begins 1:54 AM EDT
Moon enters Capricorn ♑ 5:38 AM EDT
♃ᴿ Jupiter Retrograde begins (ends Feb. 4, 2025)

THURSDAY, OCTOBER 10
First Quarter ◑ 2:55 PM EDT

FRIDAY, OCTOBER 11
➤ Moon void of course begins 11:53 AM EDT
Moon enters Aquarius ♒ 12:31 PM EDT
♇ᴿ Pluto Retrograde ends

SATURDAY, OCTOBER 12

SUNDAY, OCTOBER 13
➤ Moon void of course begins 10: 11 AM EDT
Moon enters Pisces ♓ 3:55 PM EDT

*Anoint candles or burn an oil
lamp with olive oil and a few
drops of cypress oil.*

OCTOBER 2024

MONDAY, OCTOBER 14

TUESDAY, OCTOBER 15
► Moon void of course begins 4:00 PM EDT
Moon enters Aries ♈ 4:34 PM EDT

WEDNESDAY, OCTOBER 16

THURSDAY, OCTOBER 17
Full Moon ○ ♈ 7:26 AM EDT
► Moon void of course begins 3:26 PM EDT
Moon enters Taurus ♉ 4:00 PM EDT

FRIDAY, OCTOBER 18

SATURDAY, OCTOBER 19
► Moon void of course begins 3:33 PM EDT
Moon enters Gemini ♊ 4:07 PM EDT

SUNDAY, OCTOBER 20

MULLEIN

Sprinkle mullein around your house.

OCTOBER 2024

MONDAY, OCTOBER 21
► Moon void of course begins 5:00 PM EDT
Moon enters Cancer ♋ 6:50 PM EDT

TUESDAY, OCTOBER 22
☉ Sun enters Scorpio ♏ 6:14 PM EDT

WEDNESDAY, OCTOBER 23

THURSDAY, OCTOBER 24
► Moon void of course begins 12:47 AM EDT
Moon enters Leo ♌ 1:24 AM EDT
Last Quarter ◐ 4:03 AM EST

Scary faces on Jack-o-Lanterns will protect you!

FRIDAY, OCTOBER 25

SATURDAY, OCTOBER 26
► Moon void of course begins 4:04 AM EDT
Moon enters Virgo ♍ 11:47AM EDT

SUNDAY, OCTOBER 27

SAMHAIN

*Feel the possibilities and magic in the darkness.
Create a charm bag with iron, salt, and silver to
protect your spirit as you venture into the unknown.*

OCTOBER/NOVEMBER 2024

MONDAY, OCTOBER 28
► Moon void of course begins 11:54 PM EDT

TUESDAY, OCTOBER 29
Moon enters Libra ♎ 12:30 AM EDT

WEDNESDAY, OCTOBER 30

THURSDAY, OCTOBER 31
★ Samhain (Fixed Festival Date)
► Moon void of course begins 12:57 PM EDT
Moon enters Scorpio ♏ 1:29 PM EDT

FRIDAY, NOVEMBER 1
New Moon ● ♏ 8:47 AM EDT

SATURDAY, NOVEMBER 2

Make a kitchen witch's protection charm with parsley, dill, fennel, or rosemary. Tie the herbs with a black or red string.

SUNDAY, NOVEMBER 3
► Moon void of course begins 12:51 AM EDT
Moon enters Sagittarius ♐ 1:19 AM EDT

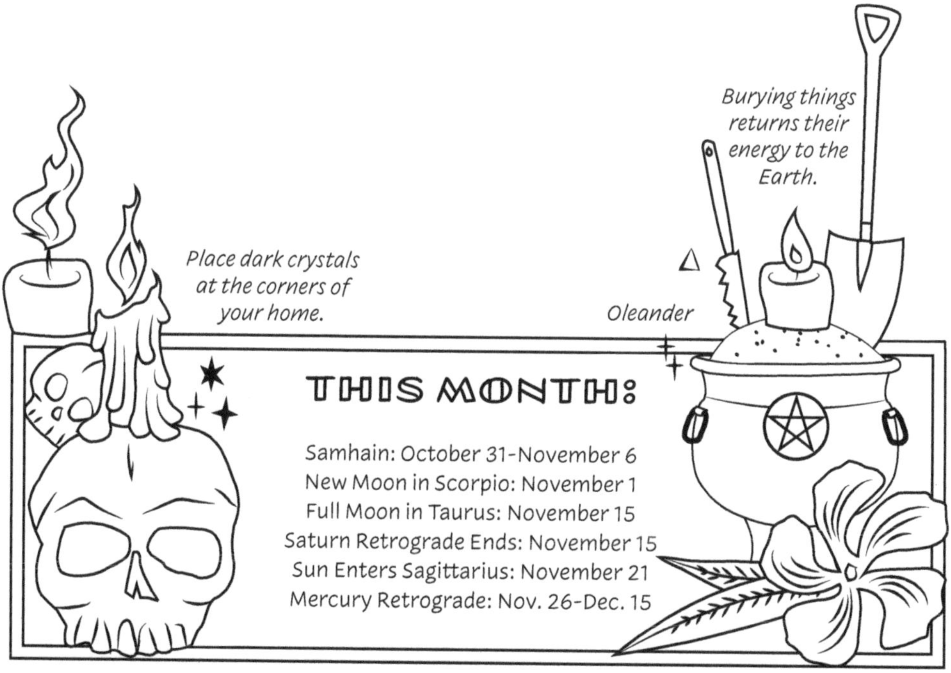

Place dark crystals
at the corners of
your home.

Burying things
returns their
energy to the
Earth.

Oleander

THIS MONTH:

Samhain: October 31-November 6
New Moon in Scorpio: November 1
Full Moon in Taurus: November 15
Saturn Retrograde Ends: November 15
Sun Enters Sagittarius: November 21
Mercury Retrograde: Nov. 26-Dec. 15

- Mystic Star -
Power of the Witch

Bats and dark creatures signify the magic of the unknown.

Heliotrope

Burning releases energy.

Four Thieves Vinegar

Anoint knives & scissors with clove oil.

Belladonna

NOVEMBER
BANISHING
Decide what no longer serves your life, magic, and intentions. Then banish them.
Clear out your physical and mental spaces.

What will set you free?

BANISHING & RELEASE
THE MOST POWERFUL SPELLS OF ALL

Banishing spells are a witch's classic! You might want to banish a thought, a pattern, a habit, or a person. However, you're actually banishing emotions and energy within yourself.

Part of banishing is surrender. This doesn't mean "to give up," but to accept what's happened. Then you can banish what you no longer desire with one of these delightful spells.

CLASSIC BANISHING: Burn things! Burning a piece of paper with written intentions or herbs with an energetic charge is simple and effective.

Or tie a natural fiber around two candles, then burn the candles until the cord breaks. You can also cut a cord or string with scissors or a sword, or imagine it in your mind's eye.

The toilet paper spell?! Yep. Write what you wish to banish on toilet paper and then flush it.

Burying things with intention (like natural paper, herbs, or rocks) will neutralize energy.

Baths and showers are also effective to release and wash energy down the drain.

Broom spells can also help to get the job done. Try sweeping energy out your front door.

For any of these spells, practice shifting your attention. First, feel and say all of your feelings. Like, "I feel ___ (disappointed, full of woe, etc.) but I intend to banish that now." Then practice shifting your attention towards what you desire.

The most effective banishing spell of all is to no longer give "it" your attention. Attention and intention are powerful magic. You might need to repeat this shift multiple times. Eventually you'll realize the energy has left your life, and you have completed a successful banishing spell.

NOVEMBER 2024

	SUNDAY	MONDAY	TUESDAY
	27	28	29
	3	4	5
	10	11	12
	17	18	19
	24	25	26

INTENTIONS
Release Your Past.

Hellebore

WEDNESDAY	THURSDAY	FRIDAY	SATURDAY
	★ Samhain (fixed date)		
30	31	1 New Moon ● ♏	2
★ Samhain 5:21 PM			
6	7	8	9 First Quarter ◑
13	14	15 Full Moon ○ ♉	16
	☉ Sun Enters Sagittarius		
20	21	22 Last Quarter ◐	23
27	28	29	30

NOVEMBER 2024

MONDAY, NOVEMBER 4

TUESDAY, NOVEMBER 5
► Moon void of course begins 5:23 AM EST
Moon enters Capricorn ♑ 10:17 AM EST

WEDNESDAY, NOVEMBER 6
★ Samhain (Astronomical Date) 5:21 PM EST

THURSDAY, NOVEMBER 7
► Moon void of course begins 5:38 PM EST
Moon enters Aquarius ♒ 5:58 PM EST

FRIDAY, NOVEMBER 8

SATURDAY, NOVEMBER 9
First Quarter ◑ 12:55 AM EST
► Moon void of course begins 7:23 PM EST
Moon enters Pisces ♓ 11:00 PM EST

SUNDAY, NOVEMBER 10

*Cast agrimony, hyssop, vetivert, or
rowan into a fire to release the past.*

NOVEMBER 2024

MONDAY, NOVEMBER 11
▸ Moon void of course begins 1:13 AM EST
Moon enters Aries ♈ 1:26 AM EST

TUESDAY, NOVEMBER 12

WEDNESDAY, NOVEMBER 13

THURSDAY, NOVEMBER 14
▸ Moon void of course begins 1:50 AM EST
Moon enters Taurus ♉ 1:59 AM EST

FRIDAY, NOVEMBER 15
Full Moon ○ ♉ 4:29 PM EST
♄℞ Saturn Retrograde ends

SATURDAY, NOVEMBER 16
▸ Moon void of course begins 2:03 AM EST
Moon enters Gemini Ⅱ 2:09 AM EST

Sweep counterclockwise to release and clear energy.

SUNDAY, NOVEMBER 17
▸ Moon void of course begins 11:09 PM EST

NOVEMBER 2024

MONDAY, NOVEMBER 18
Moon enters Cancer ♋ 3:50 AM EST

TUESDAY, NOVEMBER 19

WEDNESDAY, NOVEMBER 20
▸ Moon void of course begins 6:20 AM EST
Moon enters Leo ♌ 8:51 AM EST

THURSDAY, NOVEMBER 21
☉ Sun enters Sagittarius ♐ 2:56 PM EST

FRIDAY, NOVEMBER 22
▸ Moon void of course begins 8:15 AM EST
Moon enters Virgo ♍ 6:01 PM EST
Last Quarter ◐ 8:28 PM EST

SATURDAY, NOVEMBER 23

SUNDAY, NOVEMBER 24

To make a banishing water, mix a drop of lavender oil with spring water and salt, and leave it out under the waning moon.

NOVEMBER/DECEMBER 2024

MONDAY, NOVEMBER 25
► Moon void of course begins 12:35 AM EST
Moon enters Libra ♎ 6:20 AM EST

TUESDAY, NOVEMBER 26
☿℞ Mercury Retrograde begins (ends Dec. 15)

WEDNESDAY, NOVEMBER 27
► Moon void of course begins 4:14 AM EST

THURSDAY, NOVEMBER 28
Moon enters Scorpio ♏ 7:21 PM EST

FRIDAY, NOVEMBER 29

SATURDAY, NOVEMBER 30
► Moon void of course begins 1:19 AM EST
Moon enters Sagittarius ♐ 6:53 AM EST

SUNDAY, DECEMBER 1
New Moon ● ♐ 1:21 AM EST

DRAGON

*Use the symbolism
of dragons to
banish things.*

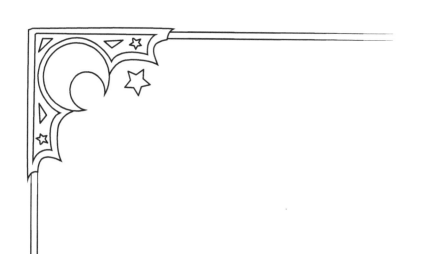

THIS MONTH:

New Moon in Sagittarius: December 1
Mars Retrograde: December 6-Feb. 23, 2025
Neptune Retrograde ends: December 7
Full Moon in Gemini: December 15
Mercury Retrograde ends: December 15
Yule (Winter Solstice): December 21
Sun enters Capricorn: December 21
New (Black) Moon in Capricorn: Dec. 30

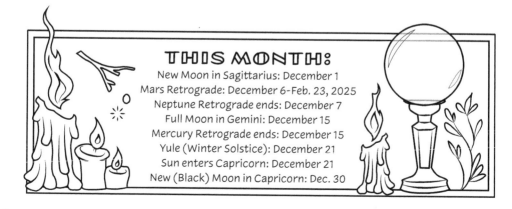

Twelve Pointed Star
Universal Energy

Sovereignty

"Only asphodels can grow
in the meadow of the soul."

- Anima Mundi -
The Soul of the World

DECEMBER
POWER OF ENERGY
Look at patterns in your life to identify
who you are in the totality of your soul.
Ask to know and follow your soul's purpose.

Roses emit the highest frequency of any flower.

Smell a rose to raise your energetic vibration.

Spiritual Evolution
Magic For Your Soul

You don't "have" a soul; you are a soul.

Spells often carry the intention of a specific purpose, usually to gain or release something.

But there is distinct kind of magic beyond that: magic with the intention of raising consciousness or evolving on a spiritual, energetic, divine, or "soul" level. Some call it "high magic." It's also known as "The Great Work" in alchemy.

It's not as lofty as it sounds because your soul (or the divine) wants to teach you about itself.

If you ask for the mystical to reveal itself—if you intend to experience it—you will find it.

RITUALS FOR SPIRITUAL EVOLUTION:

Consciousness exists through us, experiencing it through ourselves, so anything that evokes a tingling of your spine can create transcendence.

Ceremonial magic is a classic method, as performing a ritual heightens your reality.

Meditation is also extremely effective, as is chanting, humming, breath work, sacred movement (dance, yoga, kundalini)—anything that puts you in a trance-like state. Or you might prefer to work with sacred geometry or art.

So, what works for you? Experiment until you find it. Then perform that "spell" until you feel the energy rise up your spine and body. When you reach that feeling, imagine yourself surrounded by radiant, pure light. Feel this light permeating and buzzing within every cell of your being, till you feel your energy shift. Give it time and patience. You will feel it. That's the energy of the soul, and that's your magic. Put out your hands, accept that magic, and use it well. You are a soul, and you are magic incarnate.

DECEMBER 2024

	Sunday	Monday	Tuesday
	1 New Moon ● ♐	2	3
	8 First Quarter ☽	9	10
	15 Full Moon ○ ♊	16	17
	22 Last Quarter ☽	23	24
	29	30 New Moon ● ♑	31

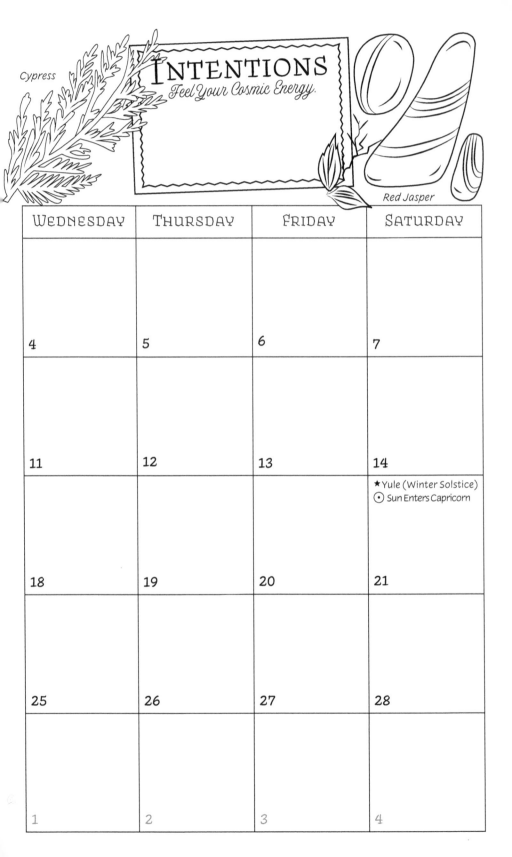

Cypress

INTENTIONS
Feel Your Cosmic Energy.

Red Jasper

WEDNESDAY	THURSDAY	FRIDAY	SATURDAY
4	5	6	7
11	12	13	14
18	19	20	21 ★ Yule (Winter Solstice) ☉ Sun Enters Capricorn
25	26	27	28
1	2	3	4

DECEMBER 2024

MONDAY, DECEMBER 2
► Moon void of course begins 10:47 AM EST
Moon enters Capricorn ♑ 4:09 PM EST

TUESDAY, DECEMBER 3

WEDNESDAY, DECEMBER 4
► Moon void of course begins 6:34 PM EST
Moon enters Aquarius ♒ 11:21 PM EST

THURSDAY, DECEMBER 5

FRIDAY, DECEMBER 6
► Moon void of course begins 7:01 PM EST
♂℞ Mars Retrograde begins (ends Feb. 23, 2025)

SATURDAY, DECEMBER 7
Moon enters Pisces ♓ 4:49 AM EST
♆℞ Neptune Retrograde ends

SUNDAY, DECEMBER 8
First Quarter ◐ 10:27 AM EST

Work with bloodstone and holly to feel peace in the present moment.

DECEMBER 2024

MONDAY, DECEMBER 9
▸ Moon void of course begins 3:45 AM EST
Moon enters Aries ♈ 8:38 AM EST

TUESDAY, DECEMBER 10
▸ Moon void of course begins 5:13 PM EST

WEDNESDAY, DECEMBER 11
Moon enters Taurus ♉ 10:55 AM EST

THURSDAY, DECEMBER 12

FRIDAY, DECEMBER 13
▸ Moon void of course begins 7:39 AM EST
Moon enters Gemini ♊ 12:22 PM EST

SATURDAY, DECEMBER 14

SUNDAY, DECEMBER 15
Full Moon ○ ♊ 4:02 AM EST
▸ Moon void of course begins 9:32 AM EST
Moon enters Cancer ♋ 2:21 PM EST
☿℞ Mercury Retrograde ends

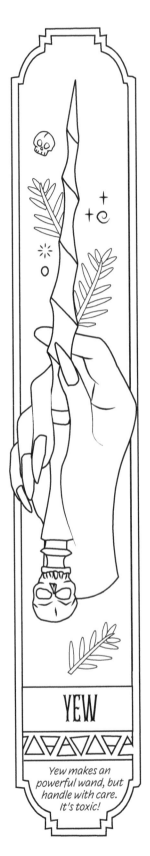

YEW

Yew makes an powerful wand, but handle with care. It's toxic!

DECEMBER 2024

MONDAY, DECEMBER 16

TUESDAY, DECEMBER 17
► Moon void of course begins 1:33 AM EST
Moon enters Leo ♌ 2:21 AM EST

WEDNESDAY, DECEMBER 18

THURSDAY, DECEMBER 19

FRIDAY, DECEMBER 20
► Moon void of course begins 12:19 AM EST
Moon enters Virgo ♍ 2:37 AM EST

SATURDAY, DECEMBER 21
★ Yule (Winter Solstice) 4:21 AM EST
☉ Sun enters Capricorn ♑ 4:21 AM EST

SUNDAY, DECEMBER 22
► Moon void of course begins 8:27 AM EST
Moon enters Libra ♎ 12:08 PM EST
Last Quarter ☽ 5:17 PM EST

YULE

*Feel the magic of peace and acceptance. Decorate
your home with herbs and evergreens to bring light
and energy to yourself in the present.*

DECEMBER 2024

MONDAY, DECEMBER 23

TUESDAY, DECEMBER 24
► Moon void of course begins 5:44 AM EST
Moon enters Scorpio ♏ 3:06 AM EST

WEDNESDAY, DECEMBER 25

THURSDAY, DECEMBER 26

FRIDAY, DECEMBER 27
► Moon void of course begins 9:24 AM EST
Moon enters Sagittarius ♐ 2:46 AM EST

*Ivy and evergreens
symbolize the
immortality of the soul.*

SATURDAY, DECEMBER 28

SUNDAY, DECEMBER 29
► Moon void of course begins 6:34 PM EST
Moon enters Capricorn ♑ 11:37 PM EST

DECEMBER 2024/JANUARY 2025

MONDAY, DECEMBER 30
New (Black) Moon ● ♑ 5:27 PM EST

TUESDAY, DECEMBER 31

WEDNESDAY, JANUARY 1, 2025
▸ Moon void of course begins 1:02 AM EST
Moon enters Aquarius ♒ 5:50 AM EST

THURSDAY, JANUARY 2, 2025
▸ Moon void of course begins 11:13 PM EST

FRIDAY, JANUARY 3, 2025
Moon enters Pisces ♓ 10:21 AM EST

SATURDAY, JANUARY 4, 2025

SUNDAY, JANUARY 5, 2025
▸ Moon void of course begins 9:30 AM EST
Moon enters Aries ♈ 2:01 PM EST

Open your doors and windows and sweep out the
energy of the old year to ring in the new.